The "CHILDHOOD HAND THAT DISTURBS" Projective Test

The "CHILDHOOD HAND THAT DISTURBS" Projective Test

A Diagnostic and Therapeutic Drawing Test

Roseline D. Davido

Translated by
Constance Greenbaum

Forewords by
David M. Abrams and
Leopold Bellak

PRAEGER

Westport, Connecticut
London

Library of Congress Cataloging-in-Publication Data

Davido, Roseline D.
The "childhood hand that disturbs" projective test : a diagnostic and therapeutic drawing test / Roseline D. Davido ; translated by Constance Greenbaum ; forewords by David M. Abrams and Leopold Bellak.
p. cm.
Translated from the French.
Includes bibliographical references and index.
ISBN 0-275-94417-4
1. Childhood Hand that Disturbs Test. 2. Childhood Hand that Disturbs Test—Case studies. I. Title.
RC473.C45D38 1994
616.89'075—dc20 93-23677

British Library Cataloguing in Publication Data is available.

Library of Congress Catalog Card Number: 93-23677
ISBN: 0-275-94417-4

First published in 1994

Praeger Publishers, 88 Post Road West, Westport, CT 06881
An imprint of Greenwood Publishing Group, Inc.

Printed in the United States of America

The paper used in this book complies with the Permanent Paper Standard issued by the National Information Standards Organization (Z39.48-1984).

10 9 8 7 6 5 4 3 2 1

This book is dedicated to
Julie E. A. Baraduc
and
Dr. Paul Darwin Davido

Contents

Foreword

Dr. Roseline D. Davido has written a uniquely stimulating and highly original book that breaks new ground in the projective drawing field, a field that has not had the introduction of any new projective approaches for over a decade.

In the United States, the standard psychological testing battery generally includes the Draw-a-Person (DAP) test, the House-Tree-Person (HTP) test and/or the Kinetic-Family-Drawing (KFD) test, which have a long literature and represent the standard, accepted projective drawing instruments employed by clinical, school, and counseling psychologists.

These tests have been found to be very useful in providing a view of how the individual perceives oneself (in the DAP drawing or the specific request to draw the self), gender identity (in how the individual may differentiate males from females in the request to draw the opposite sex on the DAP and in the KFD test) and power relationships and issues of closeness and distance with different members within one's family (seen in the KFD test in terms of which individuals are drawn the largest and which family members are drawn closest to the self drawing).

Many other individual issues, such as degree of line pressure, amount of space used to draw objects and human figures on the page, placement of objects on the page, and many other content items, provide a rich and evocative view of the drawer's passivity (light line pressure), assertiveness (heavy line pressure) narcissism (use of large amount of space on the page), feelings about belonging (placement within the group or placement of the self off to the side of the group on the KFD), personality, level of adjustment, and defense and coping style.

Neuropsychologists have occasionally employed the Draw-a-Clock test or the Draw-a-Bicycle test to assist in the evaluation of directionality, numerical sequencing, and other areas. However, these tests were developed many years ago, and the Draw-a-Clock test may even become obsolete in our more modern times of digital clocks and watches.

The Childhood Hand That Disturbs (CHaD) test of Dr. Davido is a breath of fresh air. Her instruction to "draw the drawing one used to draw when younger" is similar to Freud's instruction for patients in psychoanalysis to lay back on a couch and free associate without censure in a dimly lit room surrounded by relics of the past. Dr. Davido's drawing instruction, as in Freud's fundamental rule, immediately relaxes the person, encourages one to regress to a playful childhood memory, which may often unlock the gates to past trauma. This important drawing instruction should have very wide appeal for any mental health professional who wishes to use drawing in evaluating an individual.

In one of her most moving and dramatic examples, a totally mute six-year-old girl was unable to write; she only scribbled, and was thought of as autistic or schizophrenic. When asked to draw what she used to draw when younger, she drew two people, and with the first words anyone had heard her speak in many years, said, "My mother and me and I was three years old." With the skillful and fascinating detective work of her psychological assessment techniques, Dr. Davido was then able to uncover the fact that this child had been sexually abused at age three, and thereafter, had stopped speaking.

Another rather unusual and unconventional instruction of Dr. Davido is to ask the individual to "draw as many hands as you like," and the instruction to "draw the hand that bothers you." The many examples throughout the book illustrate that these instructions are also very revealing of inner feelings and conflicts and may be particularly useful with certain clinical populations that are often difficult to reach through the usual groupings of psychological tests, such as anti-social individuals with aggressive fighting difficulties who typically give very sparse responses to the TAT and Rorschach, and to profoundly deaf individuals, whose use of their hands in sign language is their main vehicle for interpersonal communication.

She has shown that the CHaD provides another view of the self and body image, as well as the individual's defense and coping style. In this way, it may be similar to the Draw-a-Person-Walking-in-the-Rain test, which is helpful in assessing the individual's experience of the environment as either benign (raining slightly) or overwhelming (torrential downpour), and the individual's mechanisms to defend the Self (indicated by whether or not the individual draws the person with an umbrella and, if so, how sucessful the umbrella is in keeping the rain off the person).

I applaud the introduction of this evocative new instrument from this creative French psychologist and predict that it will be of benefit to psychologists as well as other mental health professionals in their diagnostic and therapeutic work.

David M. Abrams

Foreword

The CHaD test must be seen in context. After World War II, the flow of information was often from America to Europe. In the field of testing, there was the TAT, the Wechsler, and a dozen others. Sometimes the process was more complex: Paul Schilder brought his idea about the body image from Vienna, but it was his wife, Loretta Bender, who developed the Gestalt test. The Rorschach test was also the product of interaction: Emil Oberholzer, Rorschach's friend, brought a sort of Calvinistic version of the Rorschach, not more than two or three sentences for diagnosis. It was left to Beck and Klopfer to develop a richer format, and slowly Americanization led to tests like the Minnesota Multiphasic Personality Inventory.

However, at this writing, an organization of many European test publishers is planning to virtually invade American psychology. They really hope to occupy a good part of the American test market.

Dr. Roseline D. Davido belongs to the earlier European school. Like Newton, she sat under a tree of a vacation resort, or in a jail for adolescent delinquents, and studied "hand-writings." She invited all and sundry to draw a hand, and was suprised at what all the drawings elicited—some features of which might be called expressive—others that are more properly seen as projective.

For some Americans, the CHaD test will often lack the rigors of validity and reliability. For others, it will be a welcome relief from rigidity.

Leopold Bellak

Acknowledgments

I wish to thank my mentors, Drs. Claude M. Prévost and Edwin E. Wagner. I also extend my gratitude to those who have always provided encouragement and support: Drs. Leopold Bellak, Serge Lebovici, and Daniel Widlöcher. Special thanks are due to Dr. Louis Bails, who always believed in the CHaD, and Dr. Alain Baulon. The CHaD would not have developed without the help of those who have incorporated it into their own clinical practice, in particular Dr. Danielle Krukoff and Chantal Moreaux. I am endebted to Dr. Ann M. O'Roark, Faye Dambrot, and Dr. Stephanie Z. Dudek, all of whom have helped me develop firm ties with the American community and discover American ways of life. I would also like to thank all the people at Praeger Publishers/ Greenwood Publishing Group, and in particular Lynn Flint and Andrew Schub, who guided this manuscript so skillfully through the production process.

The "CHILDHOOD HAND THAT DISTURBS" Projective Test

Chapter 1

The Development of the Childhood Hand That Disturbs (CHaD) Test

When my second book on children's drawing came out in 1976, I was invited to a vacation club to give a series of lectures on it. After the lectures, many vacationers asked me to interpret their children's drawings. I was not overly enthusiastic about doing so because the atmosphere and the circumstances were not conducive to this type of study. Nevertheless, to respond to their demands, I set up what I believed to be a challenge: I asked the parents themselves to draw. I was astonished to find that they were all willing to try. For the next three months, like good King Louis dispensing justice under his oak, I dispensed psychology under a coconut tree.

The question was how to get adults to draw. My starting point was the drawing, which was my field. I tried out a number of projective tests I knew such as the Scribble test, the Tree test, and free drawing. None of these was very productive however because the test conditions were hard to control (because of lack of concentration and outside noise), although people were cooperative. I was surprised at the amount of interest the vacationers expressed in the various instructions. Despite much mutual goodwill however, my adult subjects remained inhibited. After two days of trial and error, I finally found the key to the problem and it was a simple one: I recognized that all the adults on the other side of the table had once been children. The vacation atmosphere made it easier for me to ask each adult to produce only one drawing: the drawing they made the most when they were children.

THE CHILDHOOD DRAWING

This new instruction had immediate appeal, but on several occasions when I heard people saying, "There actually I used green, over here it was red, etc." I realized how incongruous it was to ask people to draw their childhood drawings with a lead pencil or a green felt marker. To create an atmosphere that would elicit the feeling of childhood, I provided a box of crayons and once equipped, the adults enjoyed making these drawings. They were happy to rediscover the taste of their own particular "Proust's madeleines" of their childhoods.

Since I had no interpretation grid, I simply discussed the drawing with the creators. Their drawings had captured the authenticity of genuine childhood drawings, and the recollection of their drawings also evoked a context, a specific point in time, seemingly pinpointing an important stratum in each person's life history. This specificity would later be confirmed in all the individuals (from children to the elderly, both pathological and normal) I would study, representing a crucial factor in diagnosing pathologies.

From the outset I was aware that I had material for a test, but a single drawing would not be enough. Many difficulties were involved in asking an adult, who has a whole range of other means at his or her disposition, to draw. In fact, for adults, scribbling on a scrap of paper is a way of releasing tension, allowing them to produce those little geometric shapes that look so much like spider webs, or those infinitely repeating faces or eyes. Adults draw this way in private, and not for public scrutiny. Decorum dictates that adults not make spectacles of themselves.

This experience with the childhood drawing showed me how easily individual narcissism could be flattered and brought to the surface. A second drawing in the test would have to reach out to the individual's ego directly and would need to place the person in the limelight, making him or her a star. At this juncture, I thought of a hand drawing.

THE HAND DRAWING

To make sure that the people would have greater freedom of expression in representing body image, I did not allow them to trace around their hand. I obtained as many types of hands as people. Since interpreting a single hand was difficult, I told people to draw two hands. I was surprised however when I saw people making rockets, satellites, men from Mars . . . Instead of "two hands" ("deux mains") they had understood "demain," "tomorrow," thinking I meant them to produce a drawing of the "past" (the childhood drawing) and a drawing of the future. To overcome this linguistic problem, I modified the instructions and told them to draw as many hands as they wanted. The hand is richly symbolic in both gesture and language, a symbolism that derives from one's culture and emotions. I expected these features of the hand to come to the fore. Curiously however, rarely did anyone draw the hand in positions representing these symbolic actions, and when they did so, the drawing was meant to be a caricature, such as hands together in prayer, hands reaching out to one another, hands holding a penis, hands making an obscene gesture. Quite likely they believed that the symbolic use of the hand, with its deep cultural roots, was too primary, too easy to understand, so it was repressed. Certain psychiatric cases later would show that their caricatures of hands were meant as a provocation, in which "gesture and speech are one," although in certain cases, it reflected an impoverishment of imagination and a primary level of functioning.

The hand drawing shows the hands as a genuine projection of the body. This process may be prompted by the predominant representation of the hand in the cortex and the life-size technique I use which is the only one where a part of the body can be drawn true to size (a sheet of A4 paper can contain two full-size hands).

These two drawings, the childhood drawing and the hand drawing called for a minimum of equipment and took roughly ten minutes to obtain but yielded several systematic features. Later I would collect 500 cases to compare and contrast with pathological cases. In all, the CHaD has been used on normal individuals such as those I first tested in a vacation resort, as well as in schools, prisons and detention centers for adolescent delinquents, in closed psychiatric wards, and in geriatric hospitals and rest homes.

THE HAND THAT DISTURBS

The study of pathological cases over a number of years prompted me to ask my subjects to produce a third drawing: thc hand that disturbs. The first time I saw something that resembled the hand that disturbs, I did not realizc that it had such potential. This took place about ten years ago while I was doing exploratory work on the CHaD among adolescent delinquents in prison.

One day in 1977 at Fresnes detention center, while an adolescent inmate was drawing, I was called away to the telephone. When I returned to his cell a few minutes later, the drawing did not seem to be the same one he had been working on when I left. When I asked him where he had put the first drawing, the one with the smaller hands, he replied that I must have imagined it all and that he had not drawn anything else. Convinced that he had made another drawing, I looked around the small cell which had a table, two chairs, and a closet. No drawing was in view. Next I called in one of the staff to help me find the drawing and we found it in the closet, with eight folds. There were the small hands, but now they had handcuffs on them (figure 1.1).

When I asked the boy why he had wanted to hide the drawing, he said that he was ashamed and that it was the first time he had been handcuffed. This was the first time that I saw that a hand drawing could "disturb." One instance was not conclusive however. Some time later, when working with patients in a psychiatric ward, I noted that after they had drawn the childhood drawing and the hand drawing these patients tended to make statements such as "I didn't make a fist because I don't like violence" and so on. By only asking them to draw hands, I was in some way preventing them from drawing precisely the hand they didn't want to draw. Thus, there really was a hand that disturbed in all individuals comparable to the hands with handcuffs.

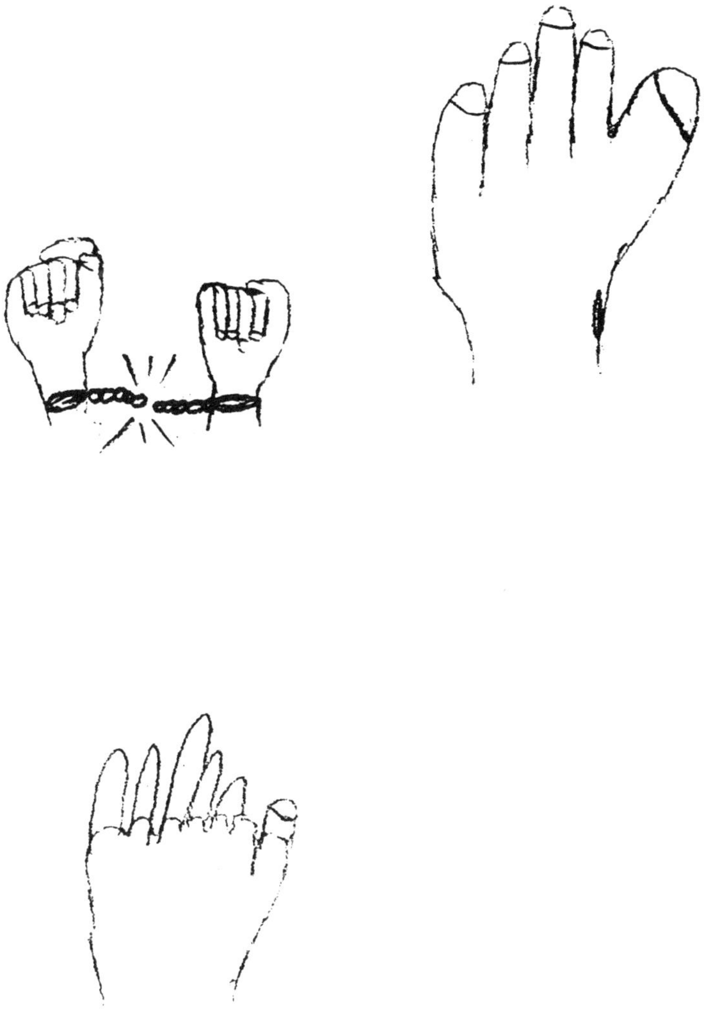

Figure 1.1
Hands with handcuffs: the impetus for the Hand that Disturbs test.

In the beginning I simply asked people to talk about the hand that disturbed. Later, when working in a mental hospital, I was struck by the fact that patients gave much importance to the hand that disturbed. It was the only one that counted, to such an extent that some patients drew one spontaneously. The contrast between the relative indifference to drawing the hand drawing and the excessive interest in the hand that disturbed was in itself revealing; that is, the hand that disturbed was the only one that was evocative. It was their hand and it was attacking them. Thus, the hand that disturbed had a real place in the test.

Thus the CHaD was now composed of three drawings. The significance of the hand that disturbs would be confirmed in a whole range of other samples. As we will see, its meaning and assessment differ for the child, the adult, and the elderly.

THE FREE DRAWING

Until 1988, I used this three-part CHaD to form a "snapshot" of the individual's life, covering the past (childhood drawing), the present (hand drawing) and possible futures (hand that disturbs). A major case in 1988 led me to add a fourth drawing. I was asked to deal with a six year old girl who had been kept back in nursery school because she was mute, and who only produced scribbles (see the case study of Elsa in Chapter 3). The CHaD showed that she could in fact draw and write coherently. Her current scribblings were analyzed and found to represent a denial of her body. The contrast between her earliest childhood drawing and her current drawings served to diagnose sexual abuse. If I had not known that this child was currently producing scribbles, I could not have been so firm in my diagnosis of a pathology. This case revealed the importance of a free drawing (FD) for children.

THE MEANING OF THE CHaD

To study an individual's personality, the three drawings (or four in the case of children roughly from the ages of 3–13) must be used in chronological order, since each drawing captures one stratum of a person's life: the person he or she was, the person he or she has become, and what he or she is afraid of becoming (The Hand that Disturbs). The fourth drawing, used with children until they cease to produce drawings as a spontaneous means of expression (roughly at adolescence) provides information on the way they situate themselves in their current world.

These three drawings (or four in the case of children) in this chronological order are revealing in that they tap areas of expression and projection that intertwine to destabilize the person and act as releasing agents. All the drawings are in fact almost free drawings since the instructions contain no references, no stereotypes, no tangible model. There is no code, and the message is deliberately kept fuzzy: the instructions call for a "childhood drawing," but make the request as a suggestion, with no stipulations as to age or specific theme. The instructions call for "hands," "as many hands as you like, in any position you like," as is the case for the hand that disturbs.

The instructions are also nondirective with regards to executing the three drawings. The examiner intervenes only if necessary and then solely to encourage the persons in the most neutral terms possible. Thus the individuals are free to express themselves. They alone define their limits, as regards themselves and others, since they know that their drawings will be judged.

The chapters that follow examine the main features of each of the drawings in the trilogy. Note, however, that the three drawings are complementary and that it is the association of the three and the comments made by the individual (during execution or in response to questions) which forms the basis for diagnosis. An individual's pathology may emerge strongly in one drawing and not in another.

Chapter 2

The Meaning of the CHaD

THE CHILDHOOD DRAWING

The first major assumption of the CHaD is that the adult person we have become coexists with the child we once were. The second assumption is that all children draw and all adults at least drew one drawing in their childhood that was particularly significant for them. It is a well-known fact that children's drawings contain a wealth of information. Drawing is a powerful means of communication for the children because they do not yet have full command of language. Drawing is thus a game, a fantasy, and a reality as well. When adults reproduce their most frequent childhood drawing (or even the one they made as a teenager), they relive their childhood contexts. The childhood environment is revealed, as are the outcomes of conflicts. After a few brief hesitations that are quickly overcome, people readily agree to draw the "drawing they did most when they were a child." Adults reproduce this drawing so easily and with so little apprehension because they have the feeling that it is really not *they* who are being examined, but the child they once were. Since in our culture no one judges a child, and furthermore since the adult has little or nothing in common with the person she or he once was, the adult can then proceed to draw the drawing that "the other" drew when he or she was young, and not perceive the situation as threatening. This mechanism enables people to regress considerably, since they no longer feel they are being judged or controlled.

This regression is probably further facilitated by the person's knowledge that the authenticity of the drawing can never be verified. Ideally, regression should give the individual confidence and provide an appropriate atmosphere for the instructions to the next drawings. The atmosphere created by executing the childhood drawing has repercussions for the conditions in which the hand drawings are produced.

The childhood drawing generally represents *ordinary situations* that illustrate scenes the person actually experienced or would have liked to have experienced. Although subjects produce multiple drawings and themes, two basic types of childhood drawings can be distinguished: *exteriors* (landscapes, houses and their equivalents) and *drawings of people.* For example, a person may draw what his father or mother taught him to draw, or the figure that appeared the most often in the drawing such as a scene with a king and a queen and a castle.

These themes in the childhood drawing can be paralleled with drawings that appeal to memory restitution or are "screen memories." The instruction "the most often" sets the stage for regression, and the person generates a psychological working-out of his or her experience of childhood in "snapshot" form. Experience shows that the childhood drawing resurfaces from the past with particular strength in individuals from all walks of life. The individual reproduces his or her body image unchanged. All these features warrant interpreting the childhood drawing along the same symbolic lines as we use when interpreting drawings made by children.

Thus, giving a person the opportunity to draw his or her childhood drawing provides a route to the past and to memories. It turns the artist into an autobiographer and makes the individual someone special, with a special history. Furthermore, it lets the person become an artist and develop his or her own form of responsiveness, because the process of executing the childhood drawing has artistic connotations. People often comment, "I added this or that to make it pretty." The aesthetic concerns of childhood are extremely important.

People tend to believe that the childhood drawing is an epiphenomenon in their lives and that only the here and now really exists, with no direct ties with the past. Freud, in the *Psychopathology of Daily Life* (1901), says that we all have memories of our early childhoods whose content can surprise us because they are made up of ordinary, day-to-day impressions that could not have produced an emotional effect on even a child's experience, but that nevertheless were noticed down to the last detail—a luxury of detail—while more or less contemporary episodes left no trace in memory. For example, Freud cites a philology professor whose first memory goes back to the age of 3 or 4. He recalls a table with a bowl of ice cream on it. In that same period of time his grandmother died, an event that, according to his parents, upset the child greatly. But the person who has become the professor of philology "knows nothing" about this death; his only memory of that period is the bowl of ice cream. Freud terms these memories "screen memories," memories that operate as though memory selected and hierarchized events in a given period so that priority to an epiphenomenon masked the major event. Absence of regression may operate in the same way, showing that everything that could have a connection with the past is organized as though it were governed by the present.

The childhood drawing becomes a stage in which the individual directs and assigns roles to each character. The childhood drawing depicts the first roles in the life of their creator: they often show different close ups, enlargement effects, zooms. As the person draws, an invasive, sometimes obsessive, theme in the form of a single character, a single animal, or object emerges in the childhood family relationship which was problematical for him or her.

The four examples shown in figures 2.1–2.4 (the Rag Doll, the Dinosaur, the Scribble, and the Clown) illustrate the importance of early diagnosis of emotional childhood disturbances as revealed by the CHaD. The details of these cases appear in Chapter 3.

Case Studies

Miss R's Rag Doll

Miss R is 90 the day she takes the test. She is a very dignified woman, wearing her white hair up in a bun. She is in a wheelchair. One of her legs was amputated as a result of circulatory problems. She uses a prosthesis when she wants to walk. She is very active. She reads a great deal and loves to knit sweaters for the staff. Miss R immediately remembers that she drew a doll and she exclaims while drawing "It's a little messed up." She then asks if she can use color in her drawing and adds, "There, I really like that."

The drawing proceeds. She makes a well-proportioned rag doll, standing firmly on its feet, arms outstretched (figure 2.1). The face has no features. She uses pastel colors to make the cheeks, hands and feet pink. The doll is wearing a blue shirtdress with a collar that buttons down the front. The doll is very harmonious.

During the interview, Miss R adds, "I was the third girl and my mother wanted a boy. I had a doll, when I turned 13, my mother forced me to take it to the Children's Hospital. Give that to children! I took care of it. Even now it hurts. I wouldn't have been sadder if I had had to give up my own child."

In an information session on the CHaD run for the hospital staff where this woman was hospitalized, the staff was extremely moved when we discussed her childhood drawings. Miss R had died several days earlier and had never talked to anyone on the staff about her drama. The staff realized with a shock that this nice, retiring woman had lived through a personal trauma during her entire lifetime without ever opening up to anyone about it.

If this woman had been able at the age of 13 to express her distress the day her mother gave her doll away, her life may have been different since this fear of "losing a child" had apparently paralyzed her, preventing her from living out a normal woman's life and having her own children. At least this is what we concluded from what this woman could express at the age of 90. The childhood drawing is thus contemporary with a time in life when everything is still possible, a period when life has not yet marked the individual, when trauma has not occurred.

Figure 2.1
The rag doll.

The Dinosaur

The notion of a turning point is also apparent in the childhood drawing of a 35-year-old woman who draws a large dinosaur with pink and blue plates down its back (figure 2.2). She recalls having drawn this picture when she was about 8 years old. In the interview she says that when she was about 8, her father attempted to caress her, a memory she had completely repressed which resurfaced during the CHaD. This discovery prompted her to start psychoanalysis, and what she believed to be a mere caress revealed itself to be a true case of sexual abuse.

The dinosaur is a prehistoric animal but is an attractive monster in this drawing because of its pastel colors. The dinosaur may be the woman herself or her father. The choice of soft colors, and the effeminate traits of the dinosaur suggest that it is the woman's body, which is desperately trying to preserve its integrity by defending itself with armor.

Figure 2.2
The dinosaur.

The Scribbles, or the Unspeakable Body

One of the youngest cases is Elsa. Elsa is 6. She was kept back in nursery school because she scribbles and is mute. I was asked to test her because there was some thought of placing her in a class for the mentally retarded. Although Elsa did not speak, she had good eye contact and made multicolor scribbles (figure 2.3). *When I asked her to draw the drawing she did the most when she was younger, she drew real people that were worlds apart from the scribbles she had just produced. She actually spoke and commented on her drawing by saying "I was 3." Later I would learn from her mother that her father began to abuse her sexually at that age. Thus the organization in time of her drawings is exactly the opposite from the normal course. At the age of 6 she scribbles, but when asked to draw as she did at the age of 3, she produces pictures that are much more elaborate than her current drawings. When she scribbles, she cannot speak; when she "regresses," she is able to evolve, progress and communicate.*

This is a case of *reverse regression*. It showed me the wealth of information that may be derived from comparing the childhood drawing of yesterday and the drawing of the same child today (termed *free drawing*). Thus, even very young children understand the instructions and are able to differentiate the here and now from the past, even the immediate past.

This stratum of a person's life, as revealed through the childhood drawing, emerges even more clearly when the theme is a *single person*. This is because identification may be more immediate, and any conflict becomes more salient.

The Clown

Z is on vacation in a vacation club. He is eager to draw because he likes drawing. Z is in his 30s, a bachelor, and seems at ease. When I ask him to draw the drawing he made the most when he was a child, he is enthusiastic because he recalls it very well: he drew a clown (figure 2.4). *Z adds that he drew it everywhere: on his notebooks, even on the blackboard when the teacher's back was turned.*

It is rare to find such an accurate and arresting childhood drawing. It was as though Z was happy to return to his

Figure 2.3
Scribbles by Elsa.

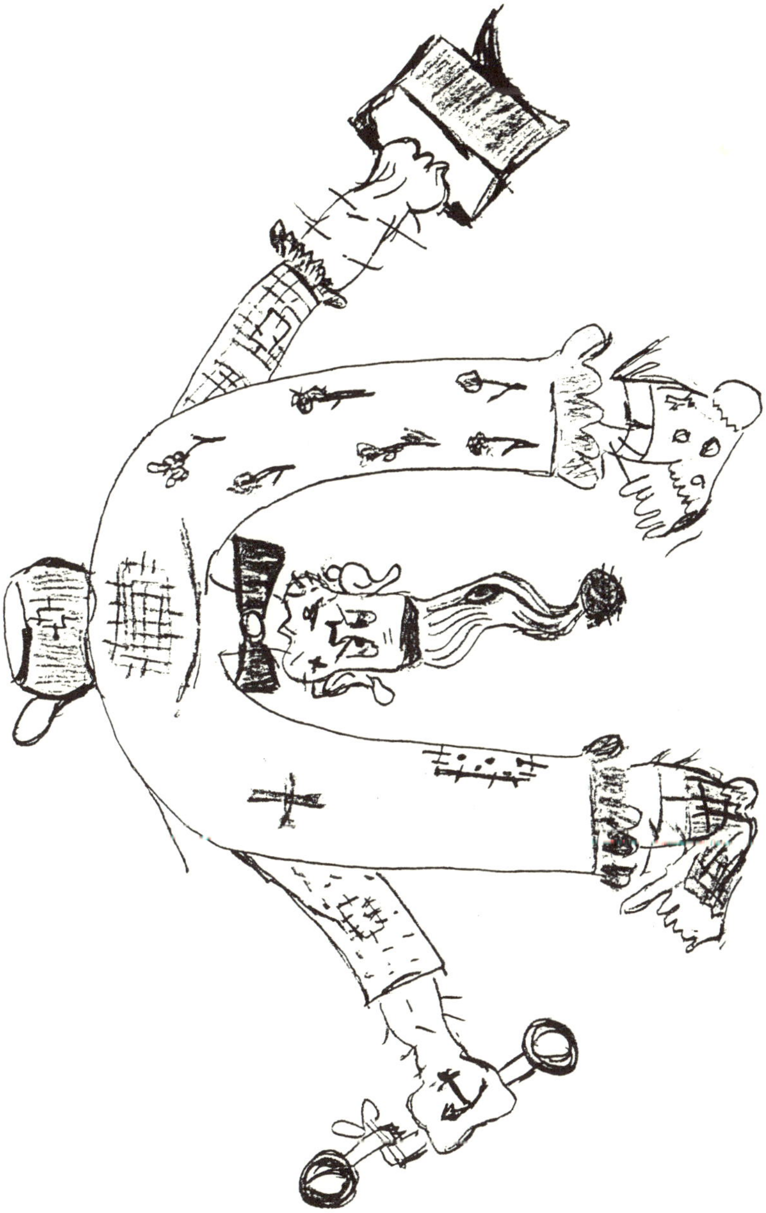

Figure 2.4
The clown.

childhood. The picture is of a clown, with his legs apart, bent over in such a way that his head, with a nightcap, is between his legs. He is holding barbells in his left hand that are broken in two and tied back together. He is holding a blue coffeepot in his right hand and has a chamber pot on top of his buttocks. As Z drew, he gave the impression that he was happy to talk about this clown, which he seemed to find handsome and positive. He drew with care, revealing a real talent for drawing.

Before interpreting the drawing, I thought that even though the clown was well done as a caricature of a clown, it probably represented someone Z knew and denigrated. This is why I asked Z if he had a brother he was jealous of. He indeed had a brother he had always been jealous of, but while explaining his sibling rivalry to me, Z suddenly understood that the devalorized person that had created problems for him during his entire childhood was his father. He told me that his father was a weight-lifting champion and that they lived in the north of France. His mother made coffee in a blue coffee pot like the one the clown is holding in his left hand. His father was very handsome. Z realized that the clown was squinting in the drawing to negate the aesthetics and the bearing of his father.

Z now commanded sympathy. The person who had come in so triumphantly now left worried to have discovered that the image he had enjoyed making fun of was in fact his father and that he was coming to terms with his father, now dead, with whom he had always been in conflict.

Thus, when people produce their childhood drawings they may realize that in fact their current lives are the outcome of this drawing, and that the problems they are currently facing are doubtless connected to their childhoods and more specifically to the snapshot represented by the childhood drawing.

For this reason, asking an adult to draw a childhood drawing may sometimes help them better analyze their childhoods, but the request is never as nonthreatening as it might seem at the outset. Behind a figure, in most cases there is a need to search out the model which is an integral part of the person's environment, even though it may not be his or her mother or father. The model can be a substitute, for

The second level is related to the features of the drawing: coherency, proportions, colors, presence or absence of details, and need for perfection. These features are examined in detail in Chapter 5.

Regression or Absence of Figurative Regression

The inability to regress often appears in childhood drawings representing houses or landscapes. Both themes are common. However, abnormality does not stem from the features or the type of drawing. What makes the childhood drawing pathological (a landscape or a house) does not stem from the fact that the individual refuses to draw or that he or she does not transcribe a theme that derives from the universe of children, but rather that the subject is *unable to regress.*

Even when the person states that he or she recalls his childhood drawing, regression appears to be impossible and the person retranscribes his "childhood" drawing as though it were a drawing he or she could make at the present time. The strokes children make, the awkwardness, the naiveness, and so forth, are absent, and there is a loss of authenticity of a child's drawing. This warrants the conclusion that the person has lost touch with his imaginary world and is totally governed by a superego that proscribes all access to regression. This is the case for people whose imaginary worlds are no longer expressed in dreams or fantasy and where all representations are banalized in words or institutionalized pictures. The person is cut off from his or her own subjectivity.

The striking feature is that pathological individuals claim to remember their childhood drawings and say for example, "I think it was a house, children always draw houses." They draw a house or a country landscape and the like, but the way an adult would draw them, by applying themselves. They use perspective, and nothing in the organization of the drawing resembles a child's drawing.

By using the stereotype of the house, the individual defends him or herself. This acts as a sort of shell the person dons to avoid revealing him or herself. What is more ordinary than a house? What child has not drawn a house, the symbol of family warmth and an ordinary childhood? In the last analysis, however, the individual is bypassed or submerged by her defense mechanisms. All returns to childhood are viewed as dangerous, or destabilizing. The person is in the grips of what is probably an unconscious fear. Why is repression necessary here? Concomitantly, why don't individuals authorize themselves to re-create the universe of their childhoods? The person is tempted to reach back to her roots, yet an antagonistic force makes her conform and turn her drawing into the stereotype of the drawing an adult makes when imitating a child's drawing.

This inability to regress is most obvious in *overly perfect drawings* (figure 2.5) which are pathological for this very reason and stigmatize the efforts of the person to fight off the threat of an imminent disorganization that is doubtless linked to hypervigilance.

People may unconsciously avoid disclosing themselves and keep their personalities secret, but they do not realize that by concealing themselves in this way they are vulnerable and that it becomes easier to define their personalities.

The instructions for the childhood drawing remove the individual somewhat from the domain of the children's drawings. Rather, we are in the domain of the adult who draws today as though he were still a child. When there is repression and/or no regression, an unconscious process may be taken to its extreme which expresses the individual's wish to be a child again, but this time a perfect child with no flaws and no problems.

When some individuals try to follow the instructions they show their willingness, but they are unable to execute the task because of their rigidity in telling the difference between who they could have been in the past and who they are now. They live exclusively in the here and now, even though they try to camouflage it by talking about their drawing as the one they did the most when they were children.

This return to childhood may re-create the conflictual atmosphere at the root of current problems and hence become impossible to draw. People may also be afraid of the idea of being overcome by feelings they may not be able to control, and rather than fall back into the style of children's drawings that they are afraid they can not bridle, they place restrictions on their own representations by drawing an

Figure 2.5
A drawing demonstrating the lack of ability to regress.

infantile theme such as a house but with an adult's style, as though they were on the defensive. When the journey back to childhood is impossible, people may also be refusing to become judges of their own childhoods.

By determining the mechanisms governing the childhood drawing, a hierarchy of pathologies can be defined. The real issue is the following: does restitution, reconstitution or reconstruction govern the drawing?

Forms of Regression: Restitution, Reconstitution, or Reconstruction

A hierarchy of pathologies can be defined by determining which mechanisms govern the childhood drawing. The three main mechanisms are restitution, reconstitution and reconstruction.

In restitution, people render what they possess. Restitution taps the emotions:

Mrs D, aged 96 says, "It was 90 years ago, how do you expect me to remember, you know at my age. I'll tell you, it was 90 years ago." As though it was the day after the July 14 national holiday, Mrs. D draws a blue, white and red flag and talks about her flag and the parade. Suddenly she exclaims, "I drew a duck, with its head a little tilted, he was flying away" (figure 2.6). *During the interview, Mrs. D says that it was a duck on the Boulogne Lake, and suddenly is very moved, smiles, and says, a little ashamed: "it's coming back now; I was with the Nuns, I had galoshes on, my classmates had patent leather shoes. The sisters banged the galoshes when we came in, it made noise. . ." Mrs. D is delighted and adds, "They dried their cornets in the courtyard at 180 avenue Victor Hugo. You make me laugh and remember"* (see Chapter 3).

Thus, people who restitute their childhood drawings remember the instances surrounding them, and the elements they add are rich in emotional tenor. Mrs. D restitutes a whole universe through her duck. This type of restitution often emerges in the elderly whose figurative drawings prompt them to confide during the interview. The childhood drawing acts as a puzzle piece that fits into the person's life history. The sole picture of a duck was connected to a whole part of Mrs. D's childhood and was the key to childhood, a

Figure 2.6
The French flag (left), and a duck (right).

period of time that Mrs. D had completely "erased" from memory, covered over with her daily worries connected to old age. The childhood drawing freed her from the overbearing present. Mrs. D's comment, "you make me laugh and remember," shows that the restituted childhood drawing brings back feelings and is an excellent starting point for exchanges.

In *reconstitution*, reestablishment takes place. In other words, the drawing is reestablished in its original form. In these childhood drawings, individuals state, "I know there was a house, a person, and/or an animal," and little by little the drawing takes shape and the drawing takes on the flavor of childhood. A true childhood drawing emerges, the trees have trunks with wide bases, the roof of the house is triangular or trapezoidal, and so on. The person needs cues to recall the childhood drawing but is able to produce a true drawing.

In *reconstruction*, people reconstruct. There is no longer a past. The individual takes measurements and establishes anchor points. I have observed this type of mechanism only in the childhood drawing in psychiatric wards, where the rational totally dominates the imaginary. In a Salpetrière hospital ward, directed by Dr. Widlöcher, a patient commented on her drawings by saying for instance, *"I was 7, I always drew a big cross. There, there was a cake* (figure 2.7). *There was also a person, it was me, sitting on a chair. There was color, red, blue, green. I was on a chair, it was me, I had a skirt on. There was a big cake, I loved sweets. I was baptized at the age of 8 because I was a bastard. The person was as big as the cross. The cake had several layers. I liked to eat, I liked charcoal pills."* Another patient, aged 62, comments, *"the cyclist's foot was twice as big as the pedal."* Another 53-year-old who comments on his childhood drawing, an algebraic construction: *"Here are the coordinates, a right angle AB, an alpha angle and a straight line that you project from this point. I don't know how to calculate the alpha angle any more; nobody knows, maybe you need Thales' theorem. It's a problem I don't ask myself constantly but often."* This need to reconstruct, to take measurements and to calculate has only been observed in psychotic patients, as shown in the "ashtray" hand drawings (figures 2.8 and 2.9) made by the same woman who produced figure 2.7.

Figure 2.7
A drawing demonstrating reconstruction. This is the Childhood Drawing by Ashtray Woman.

In psychotic patients, the childhood drawing is nevertheless experienced as a regression. At the level of the drawing technique itself, there are no signs of regression. In contrast, in other subjects regardless of age (from child to the elderly), the childhood drawing is also regressive in its execution, but above all it reflects a coherent history that is situated in a rich and variegated zone of responsiveness. The childhood drawings of normal individuals reflect an accurate and credible juxtaposition between the language of the drawing and the language of the commentary. What is remarkable is that the normal subject, even when he applies himself and con-

Figure 2.8
The Hand Drawing by Ashtray Woman.

Figure 2.9
The Hand that Disturbs Drawing by Ashtray Woman (note the dotted lines).

centrates, seems to be removed from the childhood drawing. Even when the drawing illustrates and dates a conflict, the absence of fundamental involvement shows that the subject has fully mourned the conflict, whereas the psychotic subject is rooted in it.

Perennial Conflict

In this type of never-ending conflict pathology, the individual has spent his whole childhood refining, improving, and hyperdetailing the drawing, the image of the conflict. The conflict is omnipresent, as shown in the example of the clown (figure 2.4) which illustrates this type of person-conflict dyad. It is clear that there is a persistent conflict and that the individual, by denigrating the figure (his father in the clown case) shows that he has never fully succeeded in mourning. In contrast, in the drawing of the "Black Mother" (see Chapter 3), although this woman doesn't realize that she is relating a conflict, she has always known and understood that she had a poor relationship with her mother. During the interview, she is not surprised to learn that the drawing represents an idyllic and positively valued attachment to a mother. The mother figure in the Black Mother drawing is gracious and active, in contrast to the Clown who squints, has a chamber pot on his bottom, and is in rags (a sign of denigration in children's drawings). Both of these drawings represent poor family relations, but these conflicts are expressed in radically different ways. The way the drawing is produced is the sign of pathology in the Clown drawing. The Clown was reworked, constantly redone. The Black Mother scene had not been produced before the woman was asked to make the childhood drawing.

This suggests that when the childhood drawing has marked or obsessed the individual, it loses much of its spontaneity. This can be paralleled to an interesting experience described by Pablo Picasso. "A curious thing is that I never made childhood drawings. Never. Even when I was little" (in *Picasso Dit*, Hélène Parmelin, 1966, p.86).

"When Picasso made this statement, roughly in 1965, he had been producing an abundance of drawings for the last 30 years. But he doubtless forgot this when he made the statement. From this standpoint, this forgetting shows how particularly spontaneous these drawings were, which Picasso never considered signing" (Palau i Fabre, 1966).

Inability to Define Personal Limits

The inability to set personal limits can be observed graphically or qualitatively. The absence of limits is not specifically linked to the theme of the childhood drawing, but the case of Danielle, a schizophrenic, is a revealing example of pathology (see Chapter 3). Danielle can be said to have set limits because she used the edges of the paper she used for her drawing to separate outside from inside, but she has no perception, no awareness. The medium, the sheet of paper sets the limits. The artistic qualities of the drawing should not serve as a distraction to an examiner.

Individuals who cannot set limits on the sheet of paper have difficulties differentiating the external from the internal. However, the inability to limit oneself is not always present in execution. Subjects may be unable to follow instructions: the individual makes several drawings on the same sheet of paper or on a different sheet, as though the person has forgotten the topic and has enlarged it or followed other instructions.

This qualitative criterion emerges in the case of an 18-year-old girl. She was a brilliant student with no particular problems. After a romantic breakup, however, she became melancholic and made several suicide attempts. The girl understands the instructions and comments on her childhood drawing in the following terms: "A horse with a yellow mane and tail, a tree with a hole in the trunk to let the birds come in, and then I always drew a sun." She takes another sheet without asking for permission and draws a flame and says, "If you turn it upside down it's a shark." Then she takes a third sheet and draws a sketchy, genderless figure with arms outstreched with flower hands and a flower to the right of it. This drawing is black and white, but the others are in color.

This girl did not produce the childhood drawing but rather a series of drawings responding to the impulses of the moment. Drawing a series of pictures that do not apparently respond to the instructions can reflect a weak self-image. Individuals may not be able to adhere to the theme they gave themselves when they heard the instructions.

The following is the case of a doctor who is hospitalized in a psychiatric ward. Doctor X, in his 40s, says he is a "left hander but ambidextrous." During the CHaD Doctor X talks a great deal and says that *"I was between 4 and 6 years old. I drew horses with riders, a cowboy with a mustache with revolvers who shot the enemies, he was nice"* (figure 2.10). Then Doctor X uses his right hand, draws a horse on the same sheet, and exclaims, *"It looks like donkeys, planes, a house with only one window, a tree like a cypress, roads, a path and that hill still in the background."* Dr. X comments on his drawing in the following way: *"The first plane, I was four years old, a mosaic of colors, no machine gun, I still have it, the sketch. I was furious, some others made whole villages and I was jealous. I liked green, red, bright red to dark red. And I always drew the frogmen red."*

The drawing is almost illegible because all the themes overlap: the horses' heads facing each other, a house with a mountain landscape, a plane with a series of colors, a pole, a red boat, the sketch of a diver with something red that could be an octopus. There is no regression in this childhood drawing, and nothing suggests that there has been one. Only the commentary on the drawing is recollective of an intellectual realism where the child draws everything that he knows and shows that he knows it.

Children draw this way between the ages of 5 and 7 (Davido, 1976). This individual is overcome by details, and he does not know how to choose or organize them. Absence of limits can take on idiosyncratic forms. It is always a sign of pathology in the adult.

THE HAND DRAWING

Clinical Overview

The instructions for the hand drawing, "Draw as many hands as you want," are so deliberately vague that there are as many drawings as there are artists, and a given individual rarely ever draws two hands that resemble each other. Nevertheless, in all the hand drawings, a certain number of graphic features, but above all associations emerge with a certain regularity. These can be shown to correspond to a

Figure 2.10
Unrelated themes in a Childhood Drawing.

range of individual psychological traits and to the relationships between the individual and others. Interpretation is based on the number of hands, their appearance, the relationships between or among hands, and two key features: the type of stroke and the presence or absence of color.

As was mentioned earlier, the hand is a rich repository of culturally symbolic and linguistic gestures. This repository derives from society and from individual sensitivity, but only rarely appears in the hand drawing of adults, and when it does so is typically caricatural. Hand symbolism of this type is generally a provocation, a kind of exhibitionism designed to attract attention. However, it can be the only means that very symbolically impoverished individuals have at their disposal to express themselves.

The hand drawings of juvenile delinquents are of this nature but should be assigned to a separate category. Delinquents (both girls and boys) often produce impoverished drawings: the hands often act out or parody obscene gestures such as horns or a raised middle finger. This associative symbolism is doubtless linked to incarceration, isolation, and feelings of revolt. These signs are ways of exteriorizing a form of aggressivity, but fairly primary personalities tend to produce them. The typical hand gestures that are part of most individuals' cultural "background" likely tend to be filtered out because most people see these representations as overly "simplistic" or overly easy to interpret for others; hence they repress them.

Regardless of respondent's age, impoverished drawings should not be disregarded since a hand of this type may indicate poor self-body image. A delinquent's body is in a certain way a handicapped body, a wounded and fettered one, and one deprived of freedom. Beyond the primary nature of the symbol, a fractured hand may indicate a depreciated body image in the delinquent/victim. Gesture may be a way of protecting oneself from a fear of breakdown or destruction. Later, we will see that the *hand that disturbs* is often represented as a diseased hand, a fragmented hand, reflecting a process of imminent destruction. The hands that delinquents draw are in fact a mirror image of the *hand that disturbs* in the typically normal population. Restricting the function of the hand by closing the fingers into a ball as though the fingers were mutilated may reflect the experience of suffering which the artist is trying to conceal by a provoking or obscene gesture so as to hide his or her vunerability. Thus, the obscene gesture may in fact be a gesture of modesty.

In most cases, however, hands take on a wide variety of shapes, sizes, and aspects. This immediately raises the issue of whether and in what ways these hands have a psychological significance and/or reflect a pathology.

The Psychological and/or Pathological Significance of the Hand Drawing

The sections that follow discuss the four keys to interpreting the hand drawing: the hand is a highly specialized organ, the hands belong to the examinee, there is no such thing as a realistic hand drawing, and the hand drawing is in the here and now.

1) The hand is a highly specialized part of the body: Representation of the hand in the cortex, and its motor and tactile abilities make the hand superior to other sense organs. Of all the dual organs in the body, the hands are the most mobile and the most flexible. Hands enable the body to reach or even to go beyond physical limits. In height, width and depth, hands reach out to the unaccessible.

Paul Chauchard (1970) provides a fine-grained description of the multiple functions of the hand, which he calls a motor and sense unit with a "triple receptivity to pain, pain in the hand and spreading pain" (for example, pain in the hand that accompanies a chest cold). This is only one example of the interconnections between hand and brain in both directions.

This sensitivity to pain and to bodily pain is particularly important in interpreting the hand that disturbs.

2) Hands belong to the Examinee: There is something fascinating about the symmetry and resemblance of one hand to another: hands are mirror, monozygotic same-sex twins that are part of the body and its image. Hands are a kind of severed Siamese twin because even though both are connected to the (same) body, the right hand can ignore what the left hand is doing and vice versa.

The prime characteristic of the Hand Drawing is that the examinees draw their own hands. This is due in part to the way the test was constructed and is confirmed by examinees' protocols. Clinical experience shows that individuals themselves feel the need to draw other hands, which are still theirs, but are rejected as belonging to others. This hand is termed "the hand that disturbs." It is as though the individual had not worked things out completely and needed another outlet for (graphic) expression.

In the hand drawing, people tend to personify their hands and to assign features to them. Regardless of age, in very young children as well as the very old, and regardless of drawing style, some people state they have "flat hands, they are lying there, they aren't doing anything, they are praying." and so on. These people are expressing their distress and/or depression. They are referring to their own self concepts and body images and no longer to the hands they have drawn. By talking about their hands, people place themselves in a situation of their own creation, and the hands represent this situation.

Even when people state that the hands do not belong to them, they do so unconsciously, since people assign them a function and perceive the hands as interacting with them, or they see the hands as related to their own behavior toward others or to others' behavior toward them. People's recognition that the hands they draw belong to them emerges at different levels as a function of the severity and type of pathology. The following examples illustrate that the more the fact of belonging is indirect or masked, and the hands are allegorical or esoteric, the more severe the pathology.

Daniel

Daniel, 13 and a half, is a case in point. When Daniel was 10, one of his brothers died from a bullet wound from a hunting rifle, in ill-defined circumstances. Daniel and a second brother were alone at the scene. There is doubt as to which of the boys killed the brother. Daniel is one year younger than the other brother and was placed in an institution. When Daniel was told to "draw as many hands as you like in any position," he drew one hand, right in the middle of the sheet (figure 2.11). *The stroke was firm and the proportions were correct and error free. The maturity of the drawing was striking. He stated that it was his hand. He is left-handed and placed his right hand on the table as a model. The hand had a long fairly broad wrist that ended at the bottom of the sheet. He drew nails at the top of the fingers. He used tiny "folds" drawn meticulously at the joints to produce bones. This turned the hand into a skin overlay of a skeletal frame, which emerges clearly with anatomical precision, but ends strangely in the wrist by a long crossing over of two long funereal bones.*

This hand represents the hand of the dead brother and Daniel's own anxiety transposed onto a drawing which he tried to make as anatomically correct as possible. Yet the hands present the "interpretation" as well by showing the long, crossed wrist bones that are the conventional representation of death (the crossbones under the skull). The hand testifies to deep-seated anxiety (corroborated by nail-biting) which is dominated, even masked in a rational and aesthetic representation.

In the interview Daniel states he believes he killed his brother. The hands are indeed his own hands, overlaid by the hands of the dead brother in an identification process.

Christopher

The second example is the hand drawing produced by an 8 and a half year old boy. His teacher perceives him as very smart but aggressive and fidgety in class. He draws a stick figure like the childhood drawing and hands that "aren't doing anything." When asked to draw the hand that disturbs, he bends his left hand and says that it belongs to him.

Several weeks later I had the opportunity to see this child again. He said to me that he couldn't stop thinking about the drawings he had made in my office. He showed me his wrist and said "if I had drawn a fist, you would have thought I wanted to pick a fight." I replied that that was not necessarily so and that it could mean that it was self-directed aggressivity. Christopher pretended to punch himself and said to me holding out his two fists: "I look at my hands a lot, when my mother's having a bad case of nerves, I go to the window, I make a fist and I wonder whether I'm going to jump, and then I say to myself that it would be even worse for her. I look at my fists and I wonder if I'm going to jump." (Christopher lives on the fifth floor).

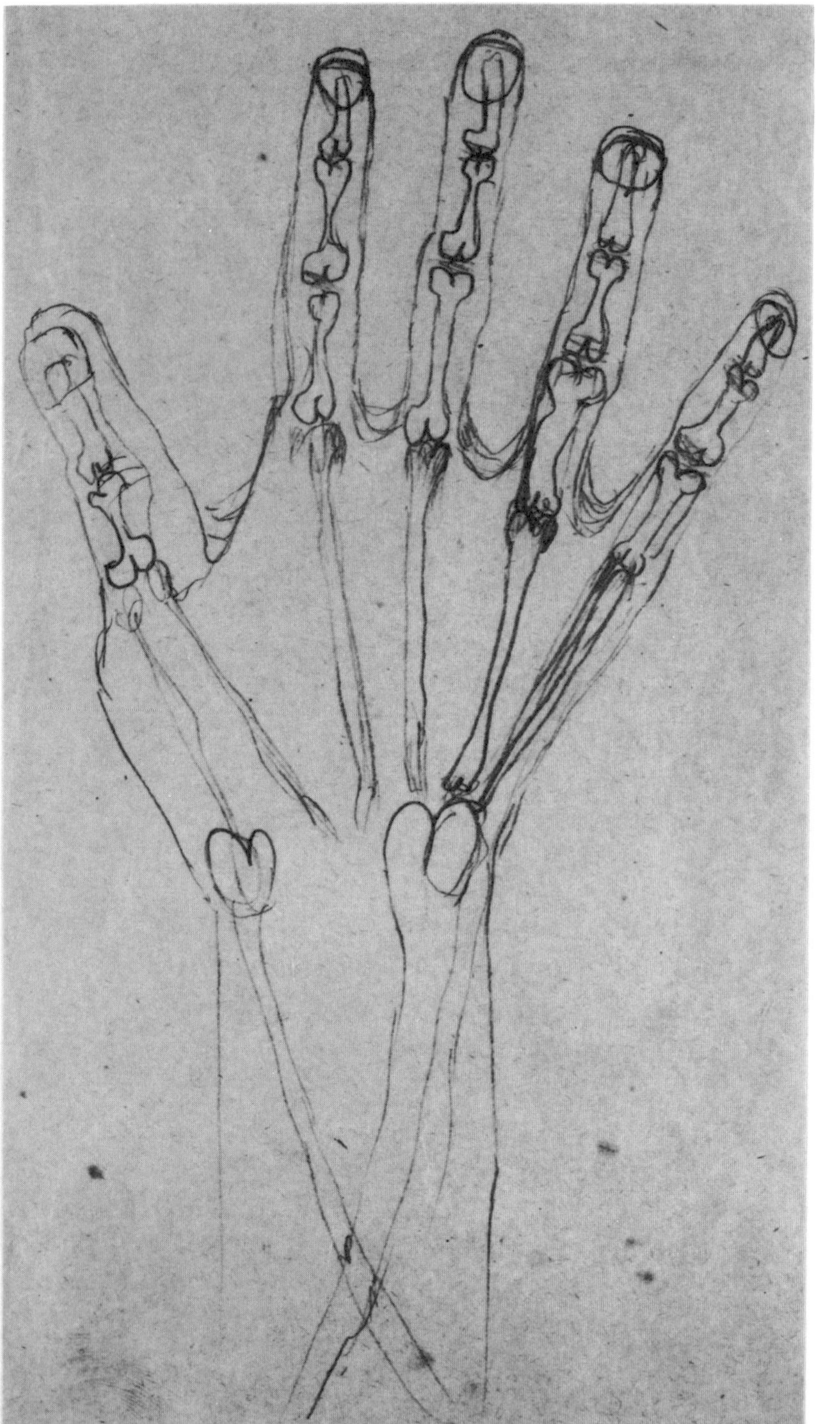

Figure 2.11
The skeleton hand drawn by Daniel.

Thus, the hands Christopher drew are really "doing nothing": his hands have six fingers, which shows that the more this child tried to control his drawing (to avoid revealing himself?), the clearer it was that he was trying to hide something. Because Christopher was afraid of appearing violent or aggressive again, since those were the reasons why his teacher sent him to me, he did everything he could to avoid drawing a fist that was symbolic of aggressivity and violence. It bothered him enough to try to interpret his drawings himself.

Thus respondents draw their own hands, and the less the hands "act out," the more revealing they are of the individual's uneasiness.

Mrs. P

Mrs. P (see Chapter 3) *was 89 when I tested her. During the interview after drawing the three CHaD drawings, she says that she drew her own hands and that they were "kaput, they don't do anything and the only thing they want to do is die." This respondent was clearly expressing her distress, which had never been apparent before. The hospital staff was alerted and modified the nature of her care.*

The 99 year old

In another instance, a 99-year-old woman (see Chapter 3) *drew hands that "did not do anything and want to die." She begged me to ask the doctor for the "last shot." But after she took the CHaD and I was about to leave, this delightful woman asked me when I would be returning. She thus projected into the future, because she was giving me another appointment, whereas a few seconds earlier she had talked about dying.*

Thus, in the case of depression, hands that are "doing nothing" are nevertheless expressive and spark reactions in their owner.

The 20 year old

In some cases it is harder to determine who the hands belong to. A 20-year-old man commented on his drawing of hands and said, "They are idiot's hands." This man constantly used the terms his family employed to describe him. He adhered to the image his family circle had of him. Other tests showed that he was not retarded. The hands that he labelled "idiot hands" indicate that he is unable to affirm or accept his personality. This indirect sign of ownership, in which the individual attributes the hands that others have assigned to him is indicative of relatively mild cases of personality disorder because there is no dysmorphism.

All these examples illustrate the fairly high consistency as regards ownership between what is produced on paper and what the individual states about the hands. In interviews people at times reject ownership. This can occur when the hands are obvious reflections of their problems. This is particularly true in the following examples produced by patients in psychiatric wards:

A woman aged 18 nervously draws three hands one after the other and says, "It's a hand that has hard work to do, it held a plowshare in its hands, it's the weathered hand of a peasant who has worked the land. The second hand is a problem hand, but tired, the third hand: the hand of a rapacious vampire."

Mrs. C, aged 43, draws three large hands (figure 2.8). The first, bent inward is "hand-ashtray made of clay" which the patient is making in another institution. The other hands are depicted from the back "with the mandatory dimensions" she states. Mrs. C tells an anecdote about the clay hand that was used for decoration in her house until the housekeeper or a neighbor used it as an ashtray when they came to water the plants. "I couldn't stand anything so cruel which made me think of torture or concentration camps" she says, and gave the ashtray to a close friend.

A 26-year-old man, M, draws three almost identical medium-sized hands seen palm up, with nails. During the interview he says that the first hand "calls the other from underground" and that the second "is work, courage, someone who won something, who raises his hand in the victory sign." The third is "death. The hand is death, someone who killed himself who lifts up his hand."

There is a certain amount of confined emotion in this description, and identification is possible only to the extent that it is pronounced in a dysphoric mode of labor and suffering. This patient perceives the hands as belonging to someone else, either human or animal. This illustrates the severity of his troubled identity and the extreme conflicts he has experienced.

Thus, in psychiatric wards, there are as many mutilated as nonmutilated hands. What is striking is the importance psychotics ascribe to the relationships of hands to working with the earth, although they are city dwellers and children of city dwellers. These patients also refer frequently to the hands as "ruined," although nothing of the sort is represented in their drawings.

Adolescents in Psychiatric Care

The following examples describe the hand drawings of two adolescents who were referred on the pretext of low academic performance.

A 16-year-old girl is suffering from arthritis and like one of her aunts, her father's sister, some deformation of the limbs has already taken place. She draws four hands and says, "These are babies' and children's hands." There is some regression in the drawing because the hands bear no signs of her disease. This girl identifies with the healthy hands of younger children where the signs of arthritis are not yet apparent.

A 15-year-old girl is suffering from a disorder of the suprenals and draws two large hands: monkey's hands. This type of disorder leads to rapid hair growth and this girl will have more body hair as she gets older. The hands, which are those of an animal, reveal to what extent this teenager's identity has been damaged.

In these cases, the hands were not described as "doing nothing" or "not belonging to anyone." These hands do not reflect depression either. Rather, they testify to identity problems and to projection of body image.

3) The hand drawings are not realistic hands: People need a mirror or the eyes of others to reflect their faces or bodies. In contrast, there is no need to contemplate the reflection of our hands in a mirror: we see them directly. This is the only image of our bodies that we can discover and perceive as it really is, with the greatest of realism. We would expect people to use their hands as models in the CHaD and to produce drawings of the hand at approximately full scale since a regular piece of A4 paper can contain one or two hands easily.

Strikingly enough, respondents, who have a flesh and blood model right in front of them, draw something else.

Projection is thus at work, since all drawings are projections of the self. The instructions to "draw as many hands as you like" does not appeal to visual perception or specifically to primary anatomical notions, but rather to pure cerebral perception. What is drawn is the felt, experienced hand: the image of a hand as generated by the brain. The hand drawing thus emerges as the reconstructed image of the body image that the subject then feels and projects as either whole or fragmented. The hand drawing is the imaginary or "spiritual" hand (in Chauchard's terms [1970]) and it is probably for this reason that people tend to draw more than one hand, and perhaps feel the need to create a "bad" one, as though they wished to reveal all the facets of their personalities.

In a few rare cases, the hands bear some resemblance to reality, and it is clear that the respondent used his or her hand as a model. I have seen only a few cases of straightfoward copying, where the hand is placed flat on the paper and traced, with no other details added. In all cases these drawings were made by the most emotionally impoverished subjects with no sense of the imaginary or an inability to tap their imaginations.

In most cases, however, realistic hands are "copies" of the hand that is not holding the pencil, seen flat, in profile, with the thumb sticking out over bent knuckles. One example is a 40-year-old woman in treatment for cancer. She draws a large copy of her hand that is well proportioned and "artistic," and then another hand of the same type but without a model. This hand is less well done and is incomplete, and is cut off by the end of the sheet. Her hand that disturbs has lost its anatomical form entirely. The hand is palm up, and is covered with crisscrossed strokes representing lines. The more this woman draws hands, the more she moves away from reality and lets go; she then enters into her imaginary world.

When realism emerges in the hand drawing, it should be interpreted as the respondent's inability to access the imaginary, or his or her excessive control over the imaginary.

4) The hand drawing refers to the here and now: In contrast to the childhood drawing, which appeals solely to regression, and in which the respondent narrates who she or he was (or would have liked to be), the hand drawing brings the individual back into the present.

The chronology formed by the childhood drawing, hand drawing and hand that disturbs drawing may unconsciously enable the examinee to reproduce a certain psychological logic, because in infancy the first self-other differentiation is achieved with the hand. The hand drawing is facilitated by the fact that the regression in the Child drawing "primes" the respondent to express his or her body image in the here and now more easily. The individual is still in the "nonjudgmental" mood created by the atmosphere of the childhood drawing.

The hand drawing is clearly rooted in the here and now because the respondent exerts *self-control*. This, however, is not compulsive repetition, but rather *creation*. This creation "sequence" is affected by the regression induced by the childhood drawing. The individual who controls his or her drawing has, in fact, already regressed. Because the individual has regressed, he or she is less vigilant, and is perhaps somewhat childlike and has somewhat less control.

Furthermore, giving respondents material that can contain reality (hands can actually fit into an A4 sheet of paper) invites them to reject constraints and may encourage extraversion.

The hand drawing can be seen as the golden rule of classical drama, uniting place, time, and action; there is unity of place: the sheet of white paper limited by its edges. There is unity of time: a hand drawing executed at a specific time, at a specific moment, after the childhood drawing. There is unity of action; and the same individual describes the action of the hands.

The hand drawing is the entry into the present, into the very instant where the hands are the here and now. The drawing captures what the hands are or are not doing. (Even when people say that their hands are not "doing" anything, this can be seen as an action.) "They take something, they move together, they say hello, good bye." They live in the present. This is the way in which the hands translate the individual's psychological present. This present is not only the moment in time but also the bodily presence, the way of being in the world which emerges through the hands.

Attitude toward hands and ownership are the key features. People draw their hands as they would like to see them or the way they would like others to see them. The next section looks at interpretation of the hand drawing in detail.

Interpretation of the Graphic Features of the Hand Drawing

The regularities that emerge in the hand drawing fall into three categories: type of hand, stroke and construction, and the use of color.

Type of Hand

Number: Drawing more than two hands is a sign of anxiety and/or narcissism. The person lacks self-confidence, and tries to depict him- or herself in as many ways as possible. These subjects exhibit varying degrees of concern to present themselves to the examiner in the best "light."

Size: Size of hands drawn is related to self image. Tiny hands express an inhibited personality, whereas a single large hand may reflect an overrated self-esteem. Most normals draw hands of different sizes. Pathology is indicated in overly large or exaggeratedly small hands.

Emphasis on Angles and Palm Lines: This emphasis is a sign of anxiety, fear of death, and at times guilt. It may be the trace of emotional trauma, as for example in the skeleton hand drawn by Daniel, but it is also seen in individuals with organic diseases.

Cutting off the Wrist or Not Drawing the Wrist: Cutting off the wrist by a line, a piece of jewelry or any other object or not drawing the wrist is generally a sign of guilt feelings. Drawing handcuffs is a good example. People may be expressing a wish to cut off all ties between their bodies and their hands. There is a need to establish a distance, and place boundaries between wishes and actions, that is, create a true separation between what is authorized and what is forbidden.

Fingers: The closer the fingers are drawn to each other, the less communicative people tend to be. People may release themselves as they would let sand rush or trickle out between their fingers. The thumb is a key feature in analyzing fingers.

When the thumb is set at a nonanatomical angle from the rest of the fingers or hand, it looks like a mass or blob that is suggestive of something primary, a major inhibition, or low intelligence.

Stroke and Construction

Stroke can be regular or irregular and can provide information on the degree of anxiety. Stroke needs to be interpreted as a function of the age of the individual, in particular in children and the very old. One particular type of stroke is apparent in schizophrenics. The line is thin, and the stroke is smooth, with no rectifications. The stroke is continuous and is made without lifting the pencil, with uniform pressure.

Use of Color

The box of colored pencils or markers that subjects use to make their childhood drawings is always made available for the other drawings in the CHaD, but few people use color for the Hand Drawing. For this reason, when color is used, it has special significance. Color should be differentiated from blackening of the nails, which is a sign of a major depressive syndrome.

In my clinical experience, color in the hand drawings has been used only by murderers or attempted murderers. One hypothesis for the appearance of color in this case is that the white sheet of paper may be evocative of a cadaver for people who have killed or have strong desires to do so. This "shock to cadaver-like white" or "white-shroud shock" may affect these individuals to the point that they use color, in an attempt to make the "mirror-image" of their crime disappear.

The presence or absence of color immediately raises the issue of *acting out.* Color in the hand drawing may be a sign of emotivity linked to major aggressive tendencies. This does not imply that people who use color in their drawings are killers, but rather that there is a strong potential for excessive violence (figure 2.12 shows the hand drawing of an adolescent who wants to be a butcher. The hands are red. Figures 2.13 and 2.14 were made in color by a teenage killer.)

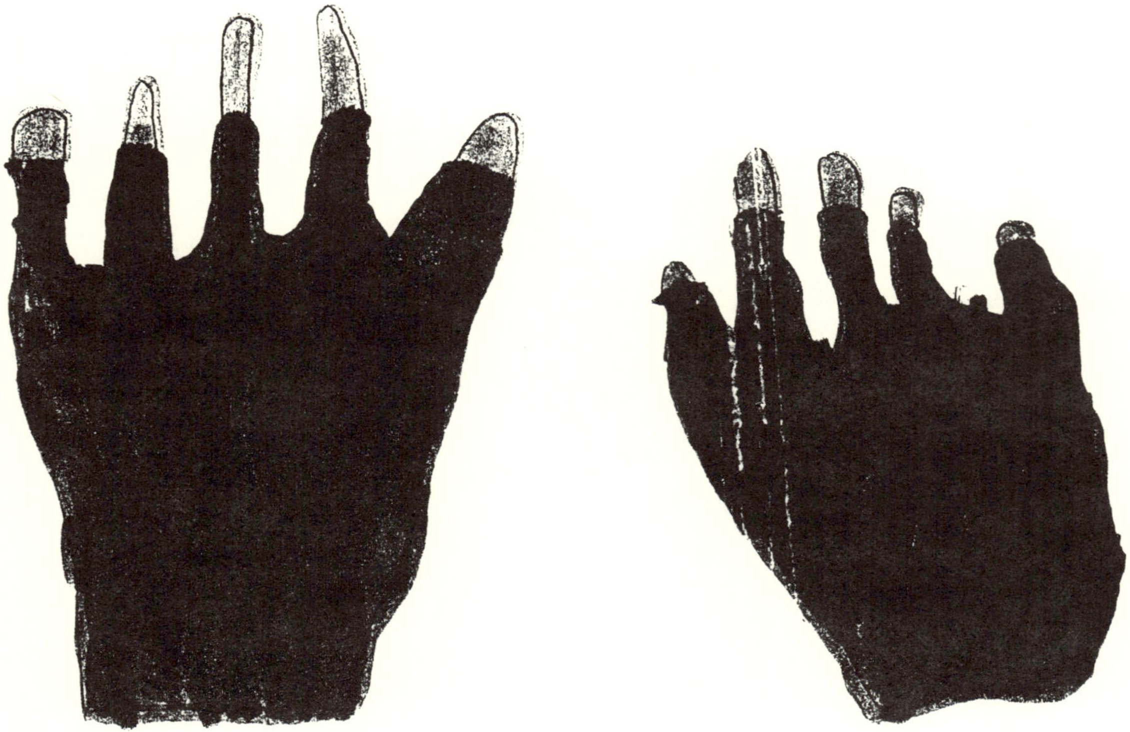

Figure 2.12
The Hand Drawing of an adolescent would-be butcher. (The original was done in color.)

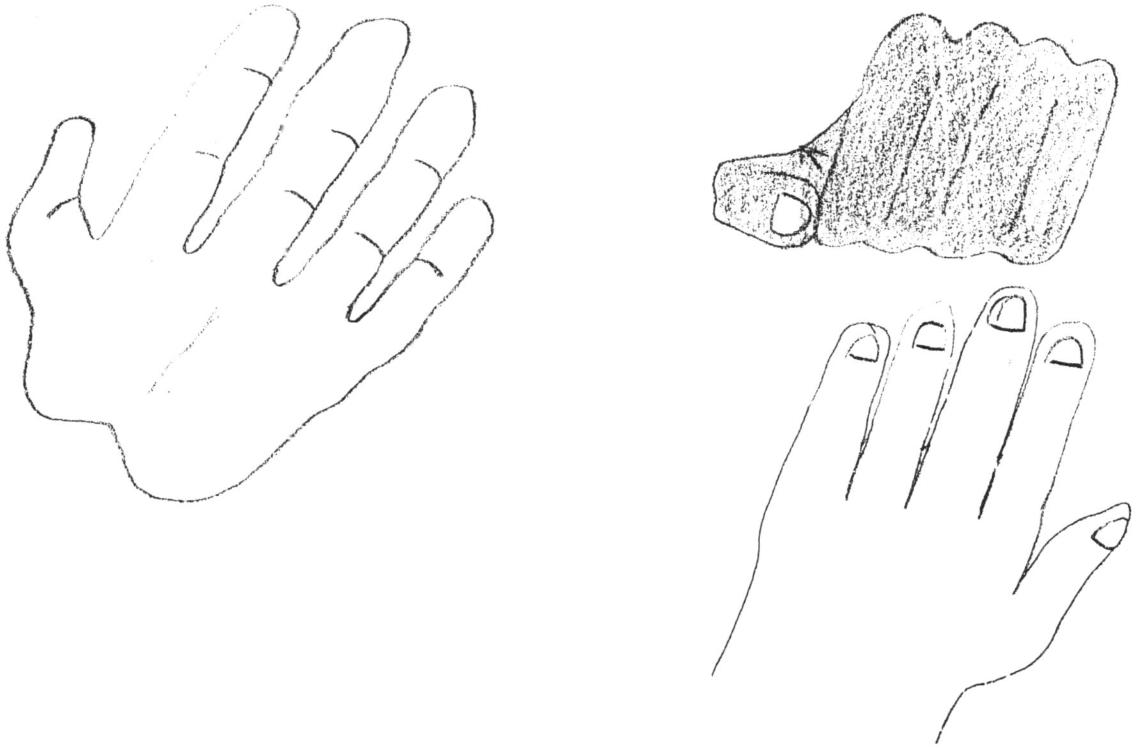

Figure 2.13
Color (in the original) Hand Drawing by an adolescent killer.

Figure 2.14
Hand drawings by the same adolescent killer.

The Hand Drawing and Acting Out

Probably no direct and simple relationship exists between color and acting out. In my clinical experience, the people who used color in their hand drawings—up to now, most have been men—had already reached the stage of acting out and had in fact been imprisoned or interned for this reason. The hand drawing was thus after-the-fact.

There are very few examples of women killers or violent women who have been administered the CHaD. In one case, a 20-year-old woman concealed her pregnancy and put the infant in the garbage after delivering in the toilet. There was no color at all in her hand or hand that disturbs drawings. The only striking feature as regards color was the use of yellow ochre in the childhood drawing and stick figures.

Another key case is that of a 16-year-old drug addict imprisoned for three murders seven years after having taken the CHaD. Was there the undetected profile of a killer in his CHaD? There was no color in the hands, but there was a balloon-head, faceless stick figure in his childhood drawing and the only color used in this drawing was dark brown (figures 2.15 and 2.16). Stick figures emerge only in the childhood drawings of individuals who have in some way encountered death.

These last two examples raise two unanswered questions: (1) Are there defining properties of the drawings before acting out and after acting out? Is color a major determinant? and (2) If so, are these defining properties more characteristic of men?

Hand drawings can be examined in infinite detail. It is more important, however, to identify themes and associations rather than focusing specifically on elementary anatomical details or circumstances. Is there a variety of hands? Are they stereotypical? Is there an impression of emptiness, or on the contrary, harmony? Is the stroke smooth? Is there use of color? To what extent does the imaginary (departures from reality) come in? The responses to these queries then need to be associated with the comments made by the respondents during the post-drawing interview when asked who the hands belong to and what they are doing.

Figure 2.15
A stick figure in the drawing by a drug-addicted killer.

Figure 2.16
Hands drawn by the same drug-addicted killer.

Thus size and the shape of the hands (fragile or robust, bony or fleshed out, even plump, etc.) are indicative of the way individuals project body image, and reveal how they represent and feel about themselves. By defining the outer limits of the hand with a stroke that can be continuous or broken, heavy or light, the person creates an envelope, a frontier between self and others, somewhat akin to what Didier Anzieu terms the "self-skin" (Anzieu, 1985). At times the frontier between self and other can also be perceived as permeable. Individuals may be so ill at ease that they let no skin show and draw a glove, "He puts on gloves." "He put on another skin because he doesn't want to recognize or cannot recognize something that belongs to him as really his own body."

Thus regardless of the way in which people execute the hand drawing, whether artistically, sloppily, or meticulously, they unconsciously reveal themselves and hence open avenues of communication. The key to the hand drawing is not the hand in itself but rather the way in which it relates to the third drawing, the hand that disturbs.

THE HAND THAT DISTURBS

Respondents are asked to make the hand that disturbs after the childhood drawing and the hand drawing. It is assumed that people have already made a micro-regression prompted by the atmosphere of the childhood drawing and that the hand drawing was produced in the carryover of this regressive atmosphere. In contrast, the third phase, the hand that disturbs, is directive, and is deliberately troubling and intrusive. It is designed to upset a carefully constructed balance. This is one of the prime factors accounting for the differences in the hand that disturbs as a function of age.

In the Adult

The hand that disturbs enables adults to reveal themselves more fully in that it allows them to deny what affects them the most deeply. The most rewarding moment for the psychologist, and perhaps the most interesting, occurs when he or she comes to understand the patient and can provide assistance as quickly as possible. The more people flee attempts at contact, the more difficult it is for the psychologist to reach out. Talking to the person about what is bothering or upsetting him or her is a way of communicating directly with him about the sense of uneasiness he or she may feel. In the hand that disturbs, the feeling of discomfort is crudely and actually there in a way that corresponds to the person's mode of functioning. The hand that disturbs captures the person's locus of suffering. The three pathological vignettes that follow are illustrative of the workings of the hand that disturbs (see Chapter 3).

A 30-year-old woman schizophrenic (Danielle) draws a hand that disturbs that is attached to the body but is perceived as an enemy hand, a persecuting hand. Apparently this patient is afraid to exist, because if she existed she would be destroyed by the hand pointing to her and desiring her annihilation.

In the devil example, a 32-year-old woman who does not speak because she is afraid to kill with words draws a microscopic hand that disturbs with claws. She defines it as her hand, that is, the hand of the devil.

The hand that disturbs of a 62-year-old man who attempted to kill his 92-year-old mother reflects an explosion of libidinal conflict. In the drawing, he designates his genitals, the part of his body that is his greatest concern and his focus of identification. It translates the violence contained within him. He exists through the suffering or pleasure of the hand that disturbs.

In these three cases, the patients all performed calculations before drawing their childhood drawings. They drew borders, and they produced what are termed "reconstructions." In stark contrast, the hand that disturbs was spontaneous, uncontrolled and uncalculated as though it involved an emotional reaction whose rapidity and strength counterbalanced the restraint and channeled the emotionality of the childhood drawing. The hand that disturbs is thus an outburst of emotion and the annihilation of the individual's entire defense system.

At what point in their histories do people begin to hide behind their wall of defenses? We have seen that the childhood drawing sometimes dates an emotional trauma, or a major change in a person's life history. The hand that disturbs is not indicative of a date, but it can shed new light on personality when associated with the childhood drawing.

The example that follows shows how the two drawings can complement each other.

A 24-year-old man draws a childhood drawing of a stick figure in the form of a rake. He then comments: "I was 4 years old and I was going to nursery school for the first time. They asked me to make a picture, and it's like an ID card for me." The hand that disturbs also depicts a rake, like the childhood drawing. How far can we trace the psychiatric disorder, mystical delirium, this patient is suffering from? What roles does the rake identity card play? What is the significance of the hand that disturbs, which represents the trace of the identity of a 4-year-old drawn twenty years later? Does the disorder go back to this time?

In contrast, normal individuals with no past pathologies tend to *distance* themselves from the hand that disturbs as though the representation was not their own but rather from the hand of someone else who has no place in the same bodily envelope. People tend to state, "It's someone else, a stranger I don't like." This generates what can be a paranoia in the form of "It's not me, it's him; it's not my hand, it's his hand: a hand that is unspeakable, castrated, with a dagger, able to kill."

In a certain way, the presence of this form of paranoia is a confirmation of normalcy. Although the hand that disturbs is clearly the respondent's hand, there is denial. This denial is the sign of normalcy. In contrast, pathological individuals immediately enter the stage set by the hand that disturbs. The hand is "inside" and they are unable to create a boundary between themselves and others. The drawing of the hand that disturbs allows them at last to obtain pleasure from pain. Psychotic patients are finally able to identify with the other him- or herself which social norms exclude from society. The emotions and pain contained in the childhood drawing burst out in the hand that disturbs. Psychotic individuals also perceive the instructions as a way to identify their sufferings, a place where pain can be enthroned.

In today's world where the successful are young, bright and handsome or beautiful, it is more than likely that someone who has self-doubts, or who is not sure of his or her level of intelligence will have trouble surviving. Paradoxically the hand that disturbs puts these people at ease because the instructions respond to a need: the need to talk about him or herself using other criteria.

Normal individuals claim not to identify either with fragmented bodies, or with a "broken" hand that disturbs. Pathologicals tend to identify completely, as was the case with the woman who made the hand-ashtray. Her hand that disturbs (figure 2.9) makes her scream because every time someone puts a cigarette out, they burn her. ("My fingers hurt and I retract them.") This patient is a good example of the overlap between the hand drawing and the hand that disturbs. She exists solely because she suffers. There is no boundary between her being and the body-object ashtray.

This example suggests that body image is a fluctuating feature, and in the case of the ashtray woman, life is experienced in terms of pain. Any outside object can become a bodily extension. In normal individuals the hand that disturbs can be depicted with equally intense suffering, the fingers can be amputated, bloody, crushed, or mutilated in a horrible way, but at no time does the person attribute or self-attribute suffering to this dysphoric, hideous hand because it apparently does not *involve* them. The hand that disturbs can produce reactions of fear and disgust, but the idea of pain is never expressed. The normal individual does not express personal suffering, the suffering of another or his or her suffering transferred to another.

One of the most common examples of the hand that disturbs in normals is amputated hands, which tend to be drawn by individuals who use their hands in their work, such as conductors and physical therapists. Their hand that disturbs tends to be handicapped, but is perceived as belonging to a person who has had an accident. The hand is not seen as belonging to the person who drew it and no idea of personal suffering is associated with it. The individual sees that the hand is injured, and at times hideous, but it remains a hand that the person describes without really involving him- or herself. In normals the hand that disturbs is described in a neutral and detached way. The hand that disturbs is an eventuality, and clearly a worrisome one, but it is not reality. In pathological individuals, the involvement is such that there is immediate theatricalization. Pathologicals "live out" their pain. This is striking in psychotics who are believed to be unaware of their surroundings, in a world of their own. The hand that disturbs enables the psychotic to experience him or herself as a suffering, plaintive individual, living symbiotic pain with the exterior (the ashtray that hurts others and self). Pathologicals and normals also differ in response latencies.

Normal individuals take their time to draw and comment on their hand that disturbs. Psychotics are in a rush as soon as they hear the instructions. In contrast to the childhood and hand drawings which do not interest them greatly, the hand that disturbs triggers a reaction. In psychotics, the hand that disturbs on paper is a trap that is closing over them. The hand that disturbs is experienced in the here and now, a painful here and now. *The hand that disturbs is not a projection but rather an extension of the self.* In normals, the hand that disturbs remains a projection of a possible future. The hand is attributed to a variety of individuals, and attribution is a means of release from the present or denial of an anxiety-producing future. *Thus, the normal individual has control over what disturbs him or her.* When designating the Hand that Disturbs, psychotics have begun to express the idea that they are fragile and unprotected, and they can finally say that they are dangerous to themselves. This suggests how important the hand that disturbs can be in prompting psychotics to begin dialoguing. The hand that disturbs may pave the way to therapeutic contact, which is so hard to establish in these patients.

As described earlier, the instructions for the hand that disturbs originated from wishes expressed by my first patients to draw the "hand they didn't draw." At first, I simply asked respondents to draw the hand they did not dare to draw, or the one they thought of when I asked them to draw hands. The current instructions grew out of this experience. In fact, respondents must handle two opposing tendencies when producing the hand that disturbs. They are engaged in a process of elimination (as were my first patients) and they are aware that the hand they draw will be judged. They tend to avoid making the hand appear "crazy."

The hand that disturbs is also a way of localizing that part of the body which is in pain or makes the person suffer. The instructions to violate societal norms and speak of one's sufferings allow people to express their most deep-seated anxieties. Crudeness in the hand that disturbs may also be a way of speaking the truth.

The hand that disturbs can engender a specific dialogue between self and self. A *duality* is set up between the self and the represented self. The hand that disturbs has its parallel in the myth of Narcissus in which man finds the revelation of his identity and his duality in the mirror: the revelation of his reality and his ideality. Regardless of which version of the Narcissus myth is used, the outcome is always the same: Narcissus dies. The same is true in mythology and folk beliefs, where death is always there when a double is present. As O. Rank pointed out, tales in which persecutory doubles appear almost always end in suicide "via the death that is wished upon one's persecutor" (Rank, 1971). Suicidal notions are also part of melancholy: "people only kill themselves after they have identified with the lost object," wrote Freud in *Mourning and Melancholia* (Freud, 1917).

Rather than the self and its double, the contradiction between being and nonbeing, flesh and dust, is the most likely articulation between self and the self-as-enemy in the hand that disturbs. A 30-year old man hospitalized for attempted suicide by overdose described his hand that disturbs as follows: *"It's punching myself, there are two beings in me."* A 35-year-old man stated: *"It's a hand in the shape of a fist to hit, bang, a violent hand, it's yourself punching yourself, I mean."* He says sheepishly, *"It's like kicking an anthill to wake yourself up."*

In these cases of attempted suicide, the hand that disturbs is perceived as their own but at the same time hostile to themselves. In other suicidal patients, there are hands that can be termed allegorical, whose main feature is their esoterism and irrationality. The next two examples below illustrate this tendency.

A 26-year-old man views the hand that disturbs as *"a troubled hand that trembles, that is afraid, it's a cosmic hand that trembles just before it turns banal, it's fuzzy, it's depersonalized, like a lizard's hand, it's a collective hand with a primitive force, it's the symbol of the liberation of the unconscious . . . it's a hand that seeks renewal, it's the symbol of fertility."* Above the hand that disturbs, this man wrote in black, *"It's a troubled hand that trembles"* (figure 2.17).

An 18-year-old suicidal girl described the hand that disturbs as *"An artist's hand whose colors come out of its fingers like a liquid."*

In these two cases the hand that disturbs was drawn in "barbed wire" fashion to give the impression of trembling. There is something more than a feeling of disturbance in these hands, and it is hard to determine what makes them disturb their creators, except for the feeling of no longer being in reality.

The key to interpretation of the Hand that Disturbs is its ownership. A horrible hand that is whole or mutilated down to one finger is perceived by both the psychotic and the normal individual as threatening. It is more dangerous to the psychotic because their own hands are perceived as the threat. The hand that disturbs can damage the psychotic, become an opponent of his body, and be a direct enemy.

In the adult, the hand that disturbs is thus indicative of the individual's relationship to his or her surroundings, and it expresses the distances and defenses that separate the person from others. Ownership by the person who drew the hand is a sign of severe pathology, and indicates that there is no distance between the real and the imaginary. Hence, no distance implies no control over emotions. The hand that disturbs is thus a prime instrument for the diagnosis of psychoses. People rarely refuse to draw the hand that disturbs.

In normals, the hand that disturbs can belong to the respondent in three cases and still reflect normalcy:

- When the person is suffering from an organic disease (such as cancer).
- When the person is undergoing analysis, where people tend to appropriate everything around them and project too easily.
- In children and in the very old who are unable to decenter from their own bodies.

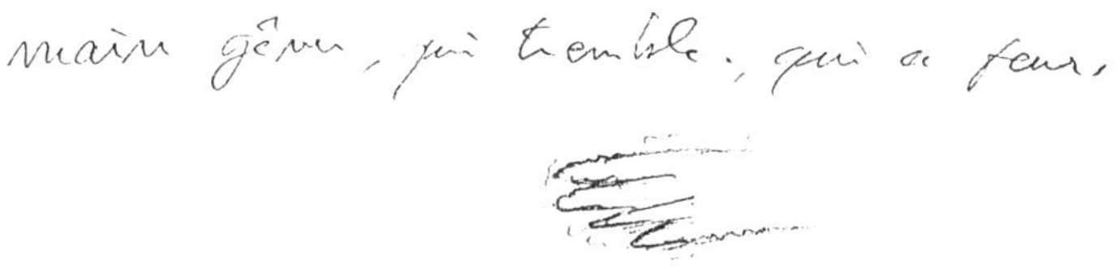

Figure 2.17
"Main gêne, qui tremble, qui a peur." (Bothered hand, trembling, frightened.)

In Children

In normal children, the instructions for the hand that disturbs are rarely perceived as a direct threat. (A right hander will say that the left hand stops him from writing well, he doesn't know what to do with it when he is writing, and so on.) When a child says that the hand that disturbs is not his or her hand, this hand often belongs to a close relative, a brother or sister. For example, a 4-year-old right handed boy says that his left hand disturbs him and adds, "My sister who is 6 goes to the big school and she writes with her left hand. She always disturbs my room." Here the hand that disturbs seems to represent sibling rivalry.

Sometimes the hand that disturbs belongs to a parent. A 6-year-old boy who looks a little sad and shy draws a childhood drawing of a tadpole-figure and then makes two tadpole figures in response to the hand instructions. When asked to make the hand that disturbs, he traces around his own hand and says, "Mommy hand, hit." This led to the discovery of child abuse, and an inquiry confirmed the child's statements. Measures were taken to place the child in foster care (see history of Kim, Chapter 3.)

In the Elderly

As is the case for children and psychotics, psychologically unimpaired elderly people understand the instructions for the hand that disturbs as a question about their own bodies and often say, "But my hands are fine, they don't bother me." The senile or patients suffering from illnesses such as Alzheimer's disease are also vigilant when they hear the instructions. The hand that disturbs is the drawing that appeals to them the most. The example that follows is taken from the case history of a 100-year-old woman who wrote undecipherable letters in response to the first two drawing instructions. On the hand that disturbs she wrote very clearly "Hands, frostbite." This woman responded in a highly appropriate way to the instructions.

Elderly people appropriate the hand that disturbs as though they no longer perceived the Other. They appear to be unable to project into the future, and everything around them seems to be related to their own bodies. In some cases, the individual's body is no longer disturbing; other people's bodies are. The hand becomes the instrument that makes the disturber disappear. The hand that disturbs encroaches upon the boundaries defined by the body.

There are no anatomical or graphic regularities in the hand that disturbs drawings. Aside from children and the very old who cannot decenter, the key is to determine who the owner is of this hand that disturbs and who by definition is persecutory. In all normal subjects, the hand that disturbs is exterior, and belongs to someone else. For all pathological subjects, the hand is theirs. Thus, this third part of the CHaD is crucial to interpretation. When the hand that disturbs belongs to the respondent, when it is consciously perceived as a body image, there is extreme likelihood that there are deep-seated imbalances in the self-concept. This diagnostic hypothesis appears to be confirmed by work described in Dr. Katherine Powell's doctoral dissertation (Powell, 1988). In this study, the hand that disturbs, because of its graphic features and above all because of the question of ownership of the hand, was found to be significantly correlated to differences in a population of 40 dysthymic versus 40 borderline patients.

THE FREE DRAWING

The free drawing, the fourth drawing in the CHaD series, is used only with children. It can be used up to the age at which children stop using drawing as a spontaneous medium of expression (at roughly about age 12–13, although individuals vary). It is interpreted in the same way as the childhood drawing. In the Elsa case history described earlier, her free drawing regressed to the point of scribbles whereas the childhood drawing was much more structured even though according to Elsa it dated back three years earlier. The contrast between the free drawing and the childhood drawings was one of the main keys for interpretation.

The free drawing can be compared to the childhood drawing in both directions. In some cases where the childhood drawing is very disruptive, it can provide some evidence that a problem has been overcome. The CHaD provides a graphic outlet for feelings and has a therapeutic effect as in the following case.

Jeremy, aged 8, was sent to me by his teacher for "dyslexia and disruptiveness. He's a dreamer." Jeremy's childhood drawing depicts two people on either side of a brown mountain. He says it is himself and his father. The mountain looks like a pile of excrement, and the two individuals are stick figures. During an interview with Jeremy's parents in the child's presence, Jeremy makes a similar second drawing. But over the course of the interview, as the parents describe their problems which Jeremy is assumed to be unaware of, he takes a new sheet and draws two people on either side of a low grassy green hill. He then takes a third sheet, and draws the same figures but this time they are on the same side of the bright green grass. In the child's presence, the parents and I explored a number of themes including marriage and relational problems. The mother, a nurse, described how hard it had been for her to watch a friend die in her ward. The parents had no idea how to communicate their existential problems to their child. In any case, the childhood drawing, which testified to a real "mountain" of incomprehension between father and son, gave way to clarification in the Free Drawing. What message did Jeremy need to hear to feel reassured and restored? In any case, Jeremy's dyslexia suddenly vanished and was no longer considered to be a "problem" in his teacher's eyes.

The free drawing, however, does not come easily to all children. The following vignette is an extreme example. I administered the CHaD to David, a 7-year-old, and then asked him to make a free drawing. He replied, in a shocked voice as though I had insulted him, "Me, draw? You must be kidding!" David was two years ahead in school and was not allowed to "waste his time drawing." Drawing was all right for nursery school, and David's childhood drawing is his nursery school one, but now he is "big." David's parents subject him to an incredibly heavy workload. Between one hour of piano practice per day, athletics, the daily "cultural" program on television, and his allergy shot every two weeks, David has no time to spend drawing. His free drawing is a beetle in bright colors, the insect used in class as a model for art lessons. Luckily, most children can still preserve this precious and useful time to draw.

Chapter 3

Case Histories

THE CHaD IN MALTREATED CHILDREN

Psychological assessments of suspected cases of abuse are extremely difficult to conduct on children. They only rarely shed light on mistreatment and hardly ever clarify the circumstances. Numerous other inquiries are always necessary. Furthermore, these children tend not to talk and in particular avoid discussing their problems. The CHaD situation is one of trust and helps initiate positive dialogue. Proven cases of child sexual abuse in children administered the CHaD show that trauma or abuse should be suspected

- When latency (time before execution of the drawings) is high for each drawing, and in particular for the hand drawing and hand that disturbs.
- When a child, after a long period of latency, does not want to draw hands. This may suggest that body image is negative and that the child may not want to disclose this "tarnished" image. The fact of not wanting to draw hands may be an extreme sign of a fragmented body image.
- When a child cuts or tears his or her drawing. Children tend to cut or tear the Free Drawing, which represents their current drawing. They are thus expressing current conflicts in their own way.

- When a child dates his or her childhood drawing. The date may not be in years and months but rather a point in time which the child experienced as traumatic or different.
- When the childhood drawing is impoverished to the point of representing only one or two figures, at times stick figures. Houses or landscapes are not represented in the cases of abuse I have dealt with.
- When the childhood drawing (the earliest in time) is well structured and contrasts sharply with current, highly regressive current drawings (the extreme being scribbles) or when the current drawings are highly geometrical.

Children's comments on their drawings are crucially important. Responses to questions about the hand drawing and the hand that disturbs (What are they doing? Who do they belong to?) are rich in potential significance.

The Hand Drawing in Children

"Hands lying down that aren't doing anything and don't belong to anyone." This is a clear-cut sign of depression. In the case of "Hands that are catching something," it is important to ask what is being caught. Often children who are victims or witnesses to violence respond in this way: "One of the hands is grasping a knife to cut meat. Hands that are hitting someone." When asked "Who are they hitting?" one maltreated child answered, "Hands that are hitting my father."

When asked who the hands belong to, however, children may reply that they are their own. Or they may state that the hands belong to everyone except the child. Here the child has not found his place in the family circle and feels unwanted. If the hands do not belong to the child, the inquiry must be extended to specify the owner since the most typical response in the normal child is child ownership. The belonging relationship testifies to the child's relationship with others.

The Hand That Disturbs in Children

Normal children typically state that the hand that disturbs belongs to them, in contrast to appropriation in psychotic adults. The hand that disturbs in children tends to be the hand that they do not use to write with, or the one they do not know where to put when they are writing. This may indicate ambidexterity or incomplete lateralization. In addition, this type of response can be found in children or young adolescents who are troubled by their bodies and have trouble accepting themselves. The hand that disturbs is often associated with a sibling, a step-parent, or any other person who (unconsciously) the child finds it difficult to relate to.

The hand that disturbs can also be "My hand, getting a knife to kill my father." "It's my hand taking a green marker; it's my hand taking a leaf, it trembles and it makes shivers." (sexually abused girl). Children from alcoholic families tend to state, "It's a hand holding a glass of water." "It's a hand hidden under the table so that you can't see what it's doing" (a case of alcoholic parents who are ashamed that their hands shake).

Children's comments should not be taken literally. Rather, they should be set within the context of the three or four CHaD drawings. The interview should not be turned into a police investigation because a child talks about a knife, a mustache, a mouth, and so on. Suspected child abuse is a difficult area because a disturbed child can also lead the psychologist down the garden path. Note, however, that it is hard for a child to maintain an incongruous story throughout the stages of the CHaD. The pictorial representation of trauma (including abuse) is never made explicit on a primary level. The child is the victim, not the agent.

CYRIL: A BOY WITH NO PLACE IN THE FAMILY

Cyril is 5 and a half, a tall, handsome blond-haired boy who looks very serious and appears to like to reason. He says right away that his father works in a restaurant where he goes to help him when he doesn't have school. He helps him peel "taters"—he corrects himself "potatoes." "Do you realize that I'm 5 and a half and I peel potatoes."

He was referred to me because he "has the impression that everybody is against him, at home, his mother thinks he acts strange . . . "

The Childhood Drawing

Cyril seems to listen attentively to the instructions and says right away that he "doesn't remember having made a drawing when he was younger." For this reason, I ask him to draw a *free drawing* and he draws a yellow car on the page horizontally with a stick figure driver drawn in overlay (figure 3.1).

The Hand Drawing

Cyril draws seven hands that look like a king's crown (figure 3.2). The hands are drawn in pencil and are average sized. He uses his hands as models and looks closely at his palm and the back of his hand. The hands are spread over the sheet: some of the fingers are pointed upward, and some downward.

The Hand That Disturbs

He draws his own hand by tracing around it, and adds a long wrist (figure 3.3).

Interview

The Free Drawing: This drawing is well structured and has a certain dynamic to it. He says that it is his mother's car that she hasn't finished paying for and that when his father gets his driver's license he will drive it and the car will be paid for. He talks about a fine that his mother hasn't paid, and money comes up frequently in his comments.

The Hand Drawing: Cyril says that the hands belong either to his mother or to his father, four to the father and three to the mother. Then he adds, "None belong to me, I don't want to live." This sheds light on Cyril's real problem: he has no place in the family.

Figure 3.1
Cyril's Childhood Drawing.

Cyril begins to talk about "the not-real daddy" his mother lives with (she is five months pregnant). He adds that he doesn't want to live or that he would rather be a baby. He says that he misses his real father and tries to give me his exact address as though I could go to his house, and says, "It's door 11." Cyril is a child in total distress.

The Hand That Disturbs: the hand belongs to his "not-real daddy" when he plays with him and the man holds him by his arms and legs upside down. For the first time Cyril doesn't use the term "my father" but "my not-real father." When Cyril is asked to talk about what bothers him and what upsets him, the real image of the "false" father emerges. What bothers him is not the hand that is playing but the image of the hand that "plays at being a father." Cyril is thus able to express one of the roots of his problems.

Interview with the Parents: the mother is a young well-dressed woman, clothed like a model, and is pregnant. The stepfather is more ordinary looking; he is short and stocky. Both seem to be very attentive during the interview. They appear to be looking for advice. The mother talks about Cyril's father in a fairly aggressive way by describing him as a "man who is better at business and earning money" than taking care of his son who asks for him and whom he is too busy to see. To avoid being bothered, he has a private

Figure 3.2
Cyril's Hand Drawing.

telephone number which his son is not allowed to have. This helps clarify the importance of money in Cyril's comments on the free drawing. Cyril is present at this interview. (I feel it is important that everything be said in front of a child, and

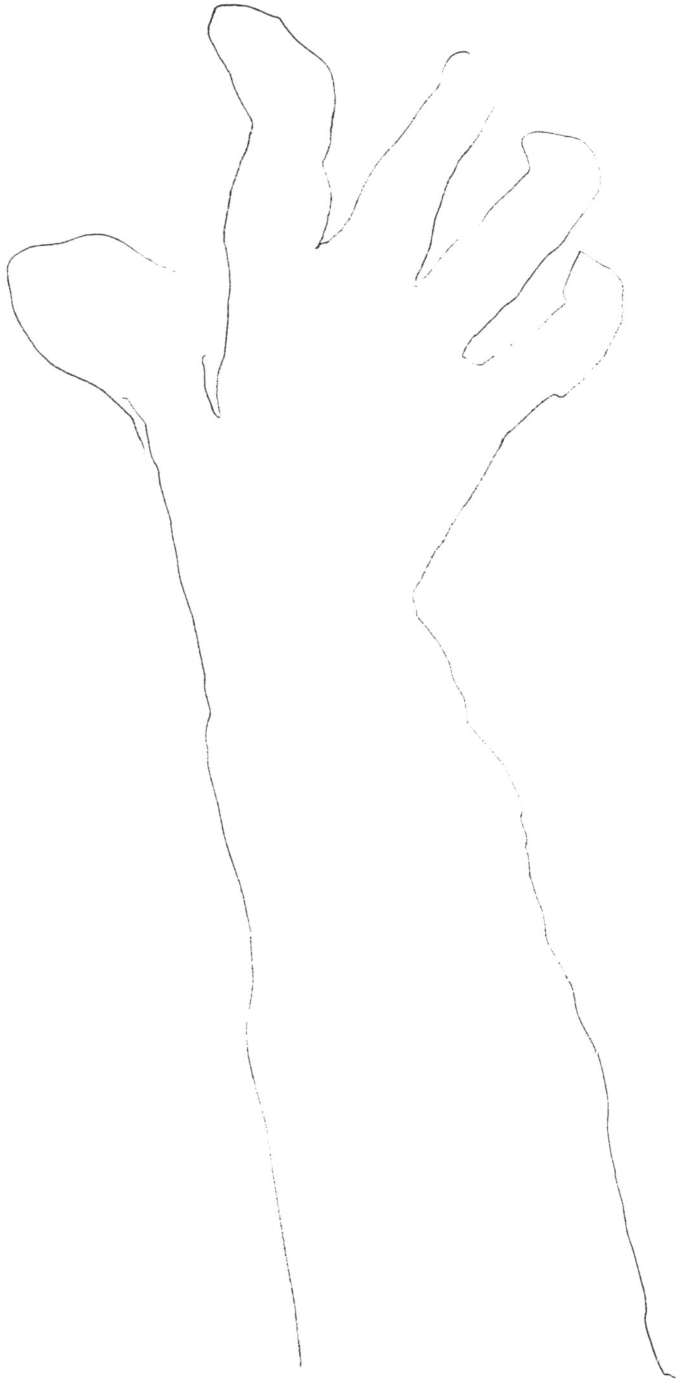

Figure 3.3
Cyril's Hand that Disturbs Drawing.

that the child can draw, enabling him or her to express affect during the interview.)

I ask Cyril if he would allow me to repeat what he said to me during the interview. He agrees and stares at his mother's face. I repeated that Cyril said he "didn't want to live." I ask Cyril if I understood and he nods his head in response. The mother seems surprised, expresses doubt, and defends herself as though a 5 and a half year old could not express himself in this way and even less so "hers." She asks to see the drawings, I show her the hand drawing and explain to her that, despite the number, none of the hands belonged to the child. In other words, the child assigned himself no place on the sheet, and I explain that Cyril's hand drawing does not exist, as though he himself did not exist. We then talk about the school Cyril attended last year. The mother adds, "Here he is in prison and even the quality of his drawings has changed. He has regressed." She tells me that according to the teacher he only draws stick figures whereas his figures were much more advanced the year before. The mother shows me a large folder of drawings carefully filled with Cyril's drawings which are good for his age, and were drawn six to nine months earlier.

For the mother, the new school is a prison and has made her son "depressive." The word is finally out. I try to explain to Cyril's parents that Cyril has perhaps not found his place in school, but he has not found it at home either. The stepfather says he loves Cyril "like his own son" and at this point Cyril throws himself into his mother's arms and says, "I want to die. When I'm 40 and you are 60, you'll be old and we can die together. I don't want to die before you." I ask him what it means to die and he says immediately, "it means you go to heaven." He looks skyward. I try to reassure Cyril and tell him that I am a psychologist for the elderly and that a person who is 100 who has an 80-year-old child still treats him or her like a "child" and gives him or her advice and takes care of him.

Comments: Cyril does not have a childhood drawing because the primal trauma apparently does not correspond to a graphic point in development for him. When his parents separated, Cyril was only a few months old. The wish he expresses when stating he wants to be a baby is in a sense comparable to a childhood drawing, to the extent that this is the last phase he lived in a pleasant way before the discomfort of the separation and the "not-real daddy" occurred.

ELSA

Elsa is 6 years old. She is repeating her last year of nursery school because she is mute, only scribbles and behaves strangely according to several successive teachers. Elsa started school at the age of 3 and no intellectual development has been observed since then.

Elsa is normal in height but looks somewhat dazed and awkward. Although she still looks like a baby in some regards, she has a "little woman" look as well. She is wearing a miniskirt and a lacy blouse.

The school is worried about her intellectual shortcomings and is considering placing her in a school for the mentally retarded. I was asked to assess her.

The Free Drawing

Because I know that Elsa does not talk and does not want to talk (eye and ear examinations are normal), I ask her to draw. Elsa draws like a much younger child, but she seems to enjoy scribbling (figure 3.4). I ask her to draw the drawing she made when she was younger.

The Childhood Drawing

With no latency, Elsa draws two fairly small female figures with long hair, wearing dresses (figure 3.5). The first figure (the tallest and largest) is on the left. The figure is oriented to the left. There is a gap between the head and the neck. The right-hand figure is leaning symmetrically to the left. The two figures look ethereal.

Her drawing is constructed with great dexterity, as though she had been waiting for someone to ask her to draw something other than scribbles. There is a scribble on the body of the figure on the right and lines on the body on the left.

Figure 3.4
Elsa's Free Drawing.

The Hand Drawing

Again with no latency, Elsa draws one large hand, with a thumb perpendicular to the fingers (figure 3.6). The hand is entirely covered with black scribbles, and the fingernail of the thumb is red. On the right there is a scribble made with a pen. The hand is extremely dynamic. The longitudinal lines on the hand give it an impression of movement.

Figure 3.5
Elsa's Childhood Drawing.

The Hand That Disturbs

Elsa again draws a very large hand, with truncated fingers forming crenelations (figure 3.7). The thumb is once again perpendicular to the fingers. There is a grey shaded area on the thumb and a curved line is drawn vertically on the hand. Inside the hand there is an embryo of a female figure and another one just below it. Elsa takes my office key which was on the table and traces around it to the right of the hand.

Inquiry

The Childhood Drawing: Elsa *talks* and says that she was 3 whereas up to then she had never said a word. She says that her drawing is of her mother and herself. She looks intensely at me. I have the impression that she feels she can be a normal girl in my presence, and not someone who is mentally retarded.

The Hand Drawing: Elsa says that it is hers.

The Hand That Disturbs: Elsa says that it is a fortress-hand, with a door and a lady who wants to break the door down. Elsa says that she has a key and shows me the tracing in her drawing. She gets up and asks me to show her how to lock a real door.

Figure 3.6
Elsa's Hand Drawing.

Figure 3.7
Elsa's Hand that Disturbs Drawing.

Comments

What is striking in this case is that a child who scribbled and did not talk, and who presented regressive behavior, was able in the space of ten minutes to produce three drawings. (The hand drawings are excellent for her age.) I had expected to find the contrary. Now I had some clues to her problems. Drawing represents body image and the scribbles were an attempt to deny current body image since at the age of 3, this child's body and her mother's body were both full-fledged entities.

The blackened hand reveals anxiety. The story that Elsa tells about the hand that disturbs shows that she feels intruded upon and she wants to protect herself by locking the door to protect the queen. The precision of the drawing and the coherency of her comments are surprising. Elsa must have a problem related to the body.

I thus asked Elsa to draw herself. Elsa draws a very large oval face in pencil (figure 3.8). She takes a brown marker and draws eyes with eyelashes. One eye has no pupil. She draws a nose and one straight line for the mouth. The face has some yellow scribbles on it. Elsa signs her drawing in blue pen.

I ask Elsa again to draw her body, in case she did not understand the instructions. Elsa takes another sheet of paper and the brown marker again and draws or rather scribbles a brown shape on the left and an empty square on the right (figure 3.9). She writes her name at the top. I was surprised not to see a figure in the drawing and I ask her to show me where the body she drew was on her own body. Elsa points to her neck as though her body stopped at neck level.

I realize that she has a physical problem. I ask her if her mother is nice to her. She seems very interested in the question and I go on and ask her if her father is nice to her. Elsa looks even more intensely at me and waits for me to ask her more questions about her father. I give her a red crayon and ask her to draw me where her father kisses her. Elsa draws a mouth over the brown mouth line and then draws a mouth with a mustache on the empty white square symbolizing her body. Almost without speaking we had found a way of communicating, and Elsa could reveal her defiled body.

Later, the mother was to confirm that her daughter had been abused by her husband at the age of 3. Elsa listens and draws a large fish with spikes. She then takes a pair of scissors and cuts it up, as do many adult and children who have been subjected to violence. Cutting or tearing are signs of the intricacies of violent relationships.

Elsa's mother was deeply in love with her husband when he left her after Elsa's birth. (There was another child three years older.) The husband returned to the wife when Elsa was 3, after having fathered a boy out of wedlock. Elsa's mother is so afraid that he will leave her again that she "gives" Elsa to him. The mother wonders whether the husband also abused his son.

Some time later, I was informed that Elsa was in therapy. I contacted the therapist to ask what he thought of the

Figure 3.8
Elsa: draw yourself.

Figure 3.9
Elsa: draw your body, and where your father kisses you.

family's relationships. He was unaware of the problem of sexual abuse and said he would inform his colleagues. Her mother recently put her in another school.

KIM

Kim is 5 and a half. He looks sickly and small for his age, and is very pale. He was referred by his teacher who reports him to be "not at the right level . . . he expresses himself poorly and infrequently." The teacher thinks he should not be sent on to primary school because he is not "mature" enough.

I was asked to assess Kim. He is very cooperative during the session and does not appear to be very interested in the extremely ordinary questions I ask him during the preliminary interview. I ask him to draw his childhood drawing.

The Childhood Drawing

Kim draws an oval tadpole man in brown marker (figure 3.10). The face has two dots for eyes and a straight line for a mouth, drawn in pink marker. The same pink marker is used to draw two legs, extending from the face. I am reassured, and I say to myself that he has understood the instructions and can regress.

The Hand Drawing

Kim draws three tadpole men (figure 3.11). One is a pencil circle with the same facial features and legs as in the childhood drawing but in black marker. The second face is round, and similar to the childhood drawing, with facial features and legs in pink. The third is drawn in brown, colored over with orange marker, and the mouth line and legs join to form an imperfect triangle. My initial impression is that Kim has not understood and will need to have an intelligence test battery.

The Hand That Disturbs

Kim places his hand on the paper and draws three hands with a pink marker and an object with a hooked shape in a

Figure 3.10
Kim's Childhood Drawing.

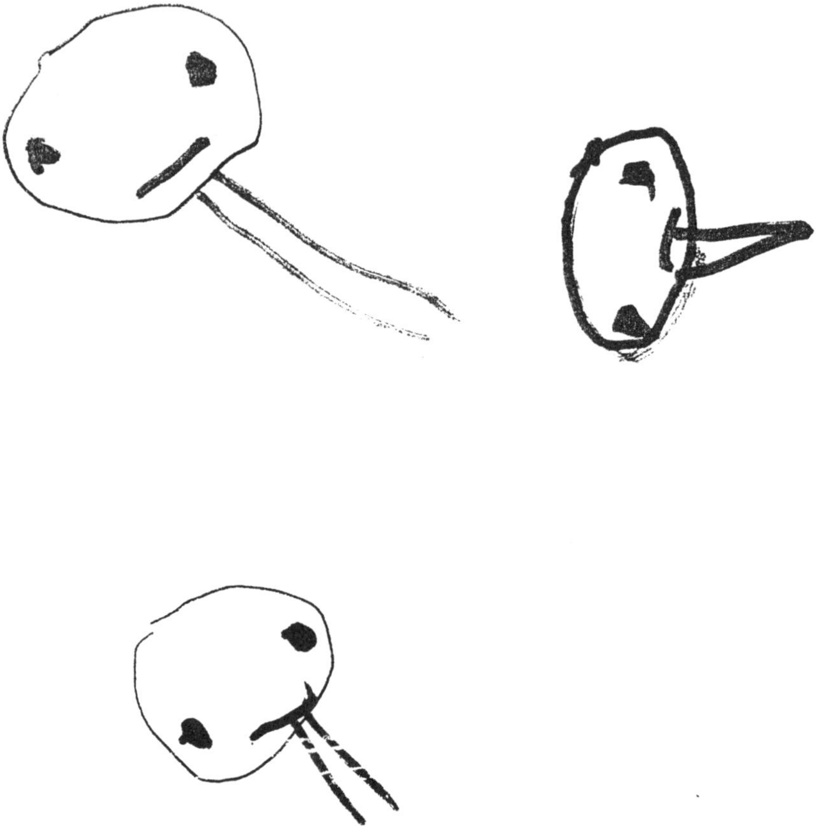

Figure 3.11
Kim's Hand Drawing.

corner (figure 3.12). The hands are large and plump with loops to connect the fingers. The hands overlap to some degree.

The Free Drawing

Kim draws an amoeba outlined in purple and green marker (figure 3.13). Inside the amoeba there is a circle and a hooked mushroom shape. The mushroom is partially black. The whole amoeba is full of tiny dots of color. Blue is used for the circle and the mushroom.

Note that Kim understood instructions only for the hand that disturbs. Perhaps the suggestion that he could feel bad, or could suffer had more meaning for him than the instructions for the other drawings.

The instructions for the hand that disturbs had the effect of suddenly eliciting the sufferings of this child who expressed no complaints of any type. The use of pink for the Hand that Disturbs probably testifies to a climate of violence that the child could not express verbally.

Interview

Kim cannot date his childhood drawing. He looks at it smiling. When asked "What are the hands doing?" he only repeats the word "hands." When, however, he is asked about the hand that disturbs, Kim says more: "Mommy's hands, hit" and starts to cry. This is how I discovered that Kim's mother, who seemed warm, was in fact an alcoholic and maltreated her son.

A medical examination was to confirm the facts, and a recommendation was made to remove Kim from his mother, who had become a real threat to him. Two years later, no court decision had been made. Although a judge had been assigned to the case and a social inquiry had been ordered, nothing had taken place. Kim was sent to me a second time, two years later, at the age of 7. His second CHaD was as follows.

The Childhood Drawing: A stick figure somewhat more advanced than the "tadpole" figure in the first drawing. A single figure is drawn.

Figure 3.12
Kim's Hand that Disturbs Drawing.

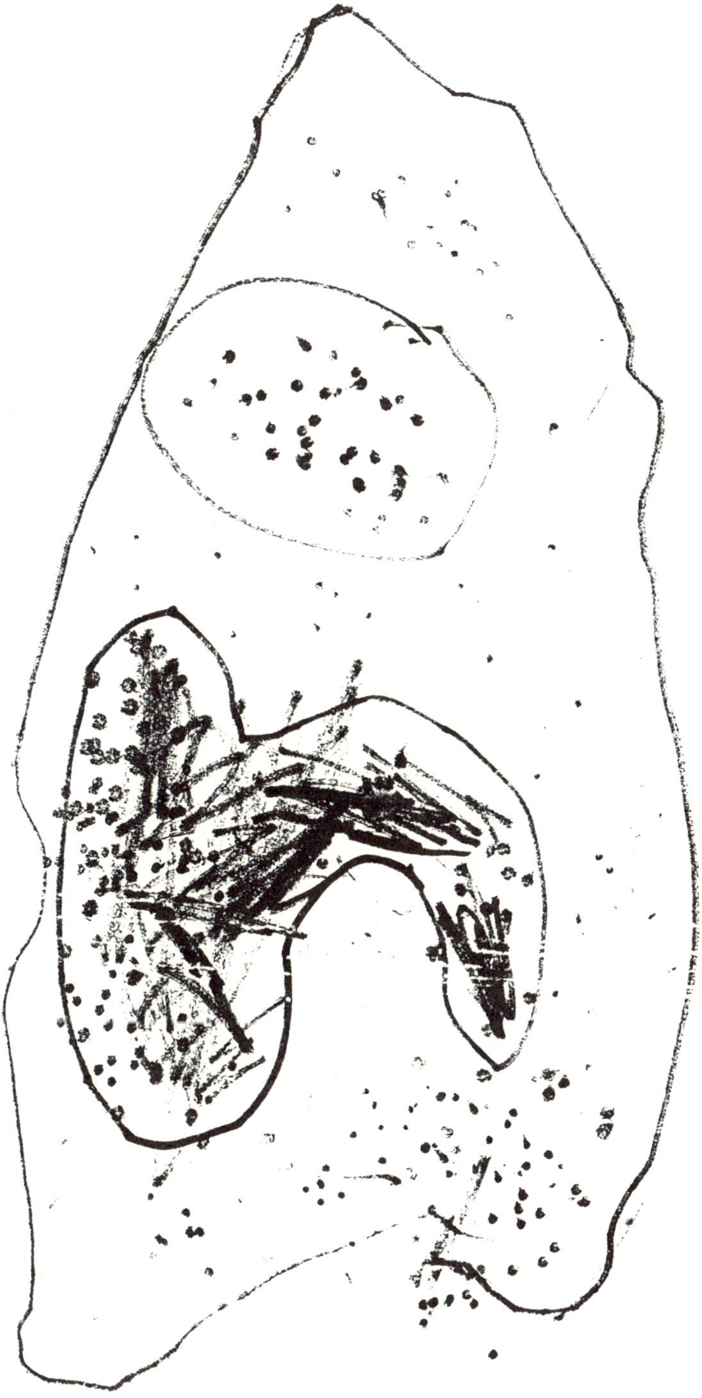

Figure 3.13
Kim's Free Drawing.

The Hand Drawing: A tadpole man, identical to the one in the Childhood drawing.

The Hand That Disturbs: Kim traces his own hand on the sheet. The hand is highly realistic and responds in an adequate fashion to the instructions.

Interview on the childhood drawing: Kim says that he often sees "men and women and sons who die of hunger on TV" and adds that he is afraid to die.

Conclusion

It was extremely difficult to determine the root causes of this child's poor adaptation since he did not communicate and was assumed to be mentally retarded. His scores on psychometric tests showed that he was borderline, but this finding was not enough to account for his behavior and learning problems. The judicial process is a long one. We can only hope that this child will be placed in better surroundings.

This case clearly shows that even when in the presence of real intellectual and emotional deficiencies, psychological aid is not be enough when child abuse is the real cause. The CHaD helped this child express his difficulties and point to the cause, a cause clearly outside the scope of psychology.

OLIVIA

Olivia was 6 years old when I first tested her. This pretty, rosy-cheeked blond-haired girl was sent to me by her teacher because she did not talk in class and seemed inhibited. Because, in addition, she had trouble learning to read, I was asked to administer a psychological battery.

At the start of the interview, Olivia hardly talked and seemed embarrassed and ill at ease. I administered the Reading Readiness test. The prognosis was good: she should be reading in six months and we were currently in November. I then gave her the Draw a Family test. She drew "a family" showing a single female character with blond hair (she states it is her mother) (figure 3.14). Then she drew "her family": again a single female figure with brown hair, in the center of the sheet. Olivia stated that it was herself. She drew grass,

Figure 3.14
Olivia: draw a family.

flowers, clouds and a sun in the top left hand corner (figure 3.15). The two drawings can be placed one on top of the other; they match perfectly.

I found it strange to have a family drawing reduced to a single figure. I asked the parents to come in for an appointment. The member who attended was the mother, a brown-haired woman who did not seem to be very young and was somewhat unkempt. The contrast between the mother and

Figure 3.15
Olivia: draw your family.

child was striking: a well cared-for blond girl with blue eyes and a very dark-haired, unkempt mother with brown eyes. According to the mother, everything was fine at home. There were no marital problems. Olivia had an older sister (five years her senior) who had presented the "same problems" at the same age but who was now "doing normally in school."

Because the mother, who worked as a cleaning lady, was clearly exhausted, I let her go without further questioning. I probably thought that what was important was the good prognosis on the reading test and that the family problems hinted at in the Draw a Family test were doubtless minor and transitory, since each of the single figures on the sheets looked satisfied, even though their arms were crossed. The fact that Olivia only drew a single figure should have alerted me to more serious problems. In addition, the perfect overlay of the drawings of mother and daughter, when they were held to the light, and the fact that Olivia drew herself as having brown hair and her mother as having blond hair should have made me react differently. However since the mother seemed credible when she said that the atmosphere in the home was a good one and that there were "ordinary squabbles, like in all families," I did not pursue it further.

Four years later, in November, I was asked to test Olivia again for learning difficulties, for refusing to participate orally in class and to talk to other children. It is rare to be asked to see the same child after so many years. I thus tested Olivia again. She had grown a lot, and her blond hair set off her angelic face. She did not answer any of my questions. She seemed extremely tired. For this reason, I administered the CHaD.

The Childhood Drawing

Olivia's childhood drawing depicts four flowers and a cactus (figure 3.16). The cactus was drawn by first making a long cylinder. She then added two leaves on each side. The drawing is done in markers, in bright colors: all the leaves on the stems are green, with the exception of the inside of the cactus, which has big red dots.

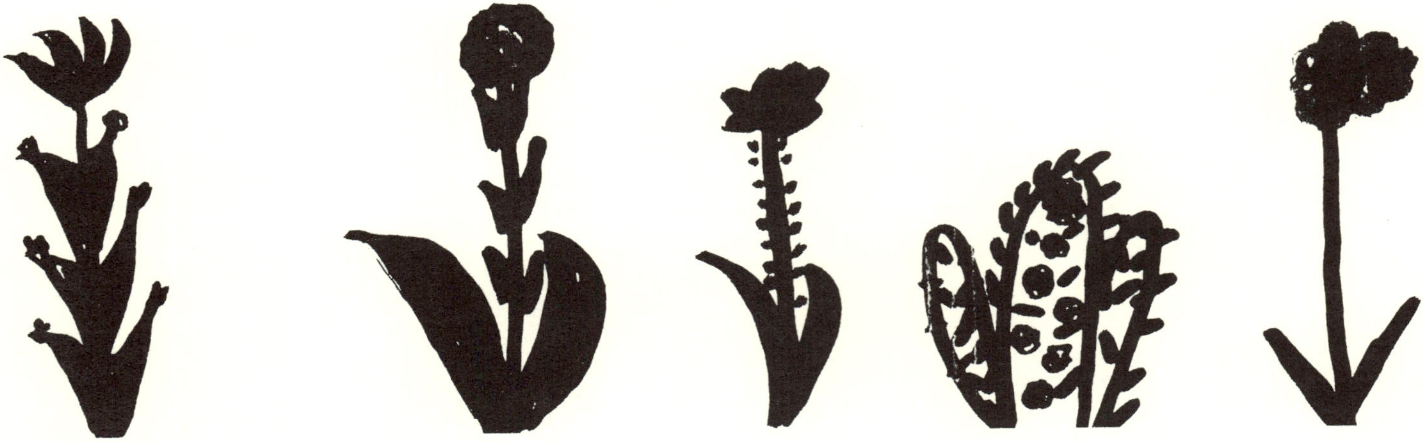

Figure 3.16
Olivia's Childhood Drawing.

The Hand Drawing

Olivia draws thirteen hands (figure 3.17), a very high number which in itself is surprising. One of the hands has the wrist split in half. All have five fingers. There are small hands, tiny hands and medium sized ones, and the fists are open. All the hands are drawn in black pencil. Some of the hands have pointed nails and others have rounded nails.

The Hand That Disturbs

Olivia classically draws her own hand by tracing around it (figure 3.18). She reproduces her hand. The stroke is homogeneous, with medium pressure. There are no embellishments.

Inquiry

The Childhood Drawing. Olivia says she was 5 when she made this type of drawing.

The Hand Drawing. She describes the thirteen hands from left to right. When asked, "Who do these hands belong to?" (individually from left to right), she answers (saying she drew her own hands):

H1: takes an object (not mine). A toy. A car
H2: (bottom left) takes something. (What?) A pencil
H3: erases the blackboard
H4: (latency) the hand that scratches (she doesn't know who it belongs to)
H5: takes a toy. A doll
H6: (latency) takes a ruler. It's mine
H7: takes a bag (not mine)
H8: takes a book (not mine)
H9: takes some money (mine)
H10: takes a flower (not mine)
H11: takes a leaf (not mine)
H12: takes a branch of a tree (not mine)
H13: takes a green marker (not mine)

Figure 3.17
Olivia's Hand Drawing.

Figure 3.18
Olivia's Hand that Disturbs Drawing.

The Hand That Disturbs: "It's my hand that takes a green marker." She corrects herself and says, "It's my hand that takes a green leaf that shakes and that makes it tremble." Finding her answer strange, I ask her what she means by trembling. Olivia gets up, brings her hands together, puts them in front of her lower abdomen, and shakes them fast while making her body vibrate.

I ask Olivia if she wants me to call her parents. Olivia looks at me in a way that can only be described as "frozen watchfulness" and spontaneously makes another drawing, without speaking, of three mushrooms, each on a separate sheet of paper (figures 3.19–3.21).

The key is the way in which Olivia goes about disguising each of the mushrooms. She first draws a cone with the red marker, then adds some folds, and at the top of each cone draws the "head" of the mushroom with two eyes, a round nose and two blue eyes with long eyelashes turned downward. She then covers the cone with a thick layer of red marker. She adds some red dots on the head of the mushroom to finish off the disguise.

I realize that Olivia revealed herself this time because she did not feel that the CHaD was invasive. Speaking little, she reached out to me and felt that she could trust me. I asked Olivia if she wanted me to ask her parents to come, in her presence. She nodded. I added, "When they come, try to help me as much as possible with your drawings so that I can ask them the questions that can help you the most."

Only the father came to the appointment. Olivia and I had agreed beforehand to focus the beginning of the interview on her learning problems. While the father was there, Olivia drew mushrooms again, with the lines crossing longitudinally. She accentuated each stroke by recoloring it in a different color, and then surrounded the whole drawing with a kind of spider web of different colors.

The father has light brown hair and blue eyes. He looks more careful of his appearance than the mother and the memory I have of her. The father gives the impression of being a "very good man," apparently he is very concerned about his daughter's academic future and I had a hard time recognizing the satyr in the message Olivia had sent me. I decided, however, to ask him a few questions, and I asked

Figure 3.19a
Olivia's Free Drawing.

him if he was very affectionate with his family, if he kissed his daughters often. The question annoyed him. He answered that he hated kissing anybody, he hated kisses and he added, "You can ask my secretaries," which was a lie since he was a building superintendent and had none. He then said, "You can come to my house to see how neat and clean it is," whereas I had not asked him any question of that sort. Thus I let him go thinking that Olivia had tricked me and that I had let myself be trapped by drawings with genitalia.

The appointment took place on a Saturday morning. Monday I called Olivia in and said to her, "Maybe your father doesn't like to kiss, he said so Saturday, but maybe he likes other people to kiss him." Olivia gave me a furtive glance and started to draw more mushrooms.

I called the parents in once again but this time in the presence of the principal. I did so because on the telephone the father warned me saying that he would only talk about his daughter's grades in grammar and mathematics. I reassured him and informed him that the principal would

Figure 3.19b
Olivia's Free Drawing.

be there to discuss pedagogy. Both parents attended the meeting.

Olivia was there and drew. The principal was talking about her grades in dictation when all of a sudden, spontaneously and without any initiative on my part, or on the part of the wife or Olivia, Olivia's father got up and said, "I know what you want to make me say: that I abuse Olivia sexually." The mother looked elsewhere naively during this outburst with no sign of astonishment. This spontaneous statement shed a little more light on Olivia's attitude.

Comments

Olivia's family drawings hinted at family problems. But because Olivia did not talk, and because what the mother had to say was apparently coherent, it was hard to identify what was bothering Olivia. What was missing was a way of communicating with her that was nonthreatening, in particular because her drawings showed such existential difficulties.

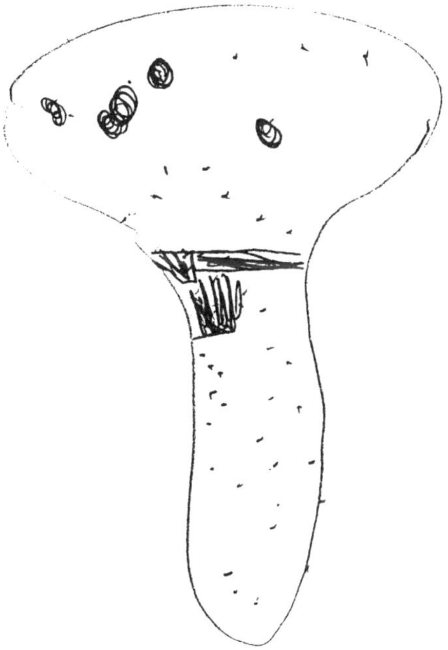

Figure 3.20
Olivia's Free Drawing.

The CHaD helped initiate dialogue. Olivia felt safe and knew that she could, if she so desired, keep her secret to herself. This probably helped her express herself. Olivia, like all children who are subjected to sexual abuse, are ashamed of themselves and their bodies. She felt guilty about having created problems for her father. I also asked Olivia to draw the Person in the Rain test. She drew a blond head with blue eyes, a large, red mouth, but no body. The figure in the rain has a similar face and no body but the eyes are different. There are no more eyelashes. She is in an anxiety-provoking situation, and her problems emerge even more clearly than in the first drawing where she has no body: she draws herself cross-eyed, the same eyes as she drew on her mushrooms.

The WISC-R scores for this girl showed normal intelligence: the scales are homogeneous and the only significant scatter is for performance on the Picture Arrangement item. This provides additional evidence for sexual abuse, since this item can provide information on the child's obedience to adult law, which here is the all-powerful father.

Figure 3.21
A drawing by Olivia done in the presence of her father.

KARINE

Karine is 9 years old. She is one year behind in school, because she repeated a year, and she is still a poor student. She is blond with long, thick hair, and is a pretty, somewhat plump girl. She is very cooperative during the session. She says right away that she has "trouble at school" and that her father slaps her when "she doesn't work well at home."

The Childhood Drawing

She draws an enormous stick figure with long blond hair and a tiny figure in the stomach identical to the large one, with blue eyes. The legs are very short and end with large black feet. The eyes of each of the stick figures are different. The mouth of the large stick figure is strikingly aggressive and is closed, with what looks like fangs.

The Hand Drawing

Karine draws two large hands that are fairly similar. The stroke is regular and is produced without lifting the pencil. There is no wrist, and a curve closes the wrist bones. The hands are empty. On each hand, one finger is very far from the others, almost at a right angle.

The Hand That Disturbs

Karine draws a single very large hand, identical to the two preceding ones, but even cruder, with the "outside" fingers highly deformed. The wrist bones are again closed and rounded off with a curved line, and the hand is also empty. The stroke is somewhat less regular for one finger.

The Free Drawing

The free drawing shows a tiny smiling female figure, which, however, is armless and is not colored, situated in a large, grey castle surrounded by a disarray of flowers, large butterflies, clouds and a sun (in bright colors).

Interview

The Childhood Drawing: Karine says that she was 3 when she drew this monster "who bothered me when I was asleep; he was in my room when I got up to go to the bathroom. I saw his shadow. He was big, and he had a baby in his stomach."

The Hand Drawing: "Sometimes they slap me. They are the monster's hand." Karine imitates what the hands do: one shows the inside and the other shows the outside. She says, "They trembled, they had a gun and the monster said to stop fooling around. My father has a gun but he never uses it."

The Hand That Disturbs: "It's the hand of boys who bother me in school. They kick me."

The Free Drawing: "A little girl, she looks at the rose, and that's the castle where she lives." Karine begs me not to say anything to her father (when I see him). She loves her father a lot, he shows her how to make babies. He explains to her that there are two fluids, but she doesn't understand. It's like the muliplication tables, it's hard to understand. She says again, "Don't say anything to my father, he'll say I'm telling mickeys." I ask her what a mickey is. She tells me that in her family it means telling lies.

The hands belong to a monster with a gun. Karine says that her father has a gun. But to protect him she says that he never uses it. The monster is clearly the father image who has been trying to teach her, as of the age of 3 or 4, about the "fluid" that is used to make babies.

Where is the mother in this story? According to Karine, she is present but doesn't interfere. The armless figure may be the mother figure, the mother who watches the scene but who Karine cannot expect help from. What Karine calls "the little girl" is also armless and her hair is blond like the monster's.

A castle is an idealized home for children who do not have the kind of home they would like. Through the CHaD Karine was able to express herself. Karine realizes that her father is the "monster." Tests such as the Draw-a-Family and Draw-Your-Family conducted three years previously revealed no sign of sexual abuse; it is now clear that she had been abused from the age of 4.

THE CHaD IN ADOLESCENTS

Adolescence is probably the most difficult period to describe or circumscribe since adolescence itself is a multifaceted transitional phase that can start as early as age 10, and can last into the 20s. These transitions are especially difficult in Western societies, where physiological transformations are so rapid that they can lead to psychological problems. Adolescents undergo true metamorphoses and like to hear others say that they are unrecognizable. But can adolescents recognize themselves?

The self and the self-image are also affected by adolescent growth. This is why it is so difficult to make clear-cut classifications of adolescent drawings in the CHaD. There is little difference between the CHaD drawings of adolescents imprisoned for crimes and those of normal adolescents. The only striking disparity is the presence of color in the hands of delinquents, and childhood drawings that are somewhat more pornographic. My feeling is that these crude, pornographic-type drawings (naked women, etc.) by jailed adolescents can reflect sexual disturbances but are primarily signs of loss of freedom.

The Childhood Drawing

In adolescents, the childhood drawing can seem crude. These drawings reflect current concerns and serve as catharsis for the feelings of sexual aggressiveness that underlie nakedness and/or provocation.

Adolescents tend to draw houses by using another pencil as a ruler, as though the home, the symbol of the family, needed to be built artificially. The faces they draw tend to be bodiless, as though the body had been expulsed. In delinquents, this unrepresented body image may also be linked to past incestuous relationships since their bodies are doubly associated with shame: shame of incest and shame as regards their adolescent bodies.

The childhood drawing of one 15-year-old female delinquent depicts a house-castle colored brown and traced with a pencil used as a ruler. There are red polka-dot curtains in the windows. Next to the castle there are two faces drawn in brown crayon, each of whom is wearing a crown. "It's a king and a queen, the king has just whacked the queen." And there is indeed a large red spot on the queen's face. The dysphoric climate tells much about the quality of her relationships to her parents. She idealized them once, making them into a king and a queen, but then they rapidly lost their royal fairy-tale attributes and fall back into the reality of a "whack."

In the normal adolescent, the childhood drawing is often highly geometrical or depicts geometrical figures. There is apparently a need to draw and align strokes. Colors tend to be applied liberally, and there are few nuances. This probably reflects the adolescent's need for structuration.

The Hand Drawing

A statistically larger number of hands are found in adolescent hand drawings than in the other categories of individuals (children, adults, or the elderly). This may imply difficulties in self-image, an attempt on the part of adolescents to show all the facets of their personalities, and hesitation as to which facet is really theirs.

Adolescent hand drawings also contain the highest number of *active* hands: the hand either imitates signs or letters (such as the V for victory) or holds something. Hands in adolescent wrongdoers tend to be more suggestive and obscene. Imprisoned adolescents tend to draw hands holding guns, a soccer ball, a paintbrush, a pencil; in short, anything phallic or with more general sexual connotations. These adolescents tend to be sexually disturbed. The case history of H, a 15 year old who produced this type of drawing is typical (figure 3.22). H served as a sexual initiator for his friends for several months. Some complexity was involved because he was apparently an investigator of practices such as fellation and sodomy. He was a peeping Tom more than a participant. His comments on his drawings were similar to those produced by abused children. This may be part of a vicious circle of violent parents breeding violent children.

In adolescents these signs are hinted at rather than blatant as is the case in psychotics. Color in the hand drawing appears only in violent adolescents (see Chapter 5).

The Hand That Disturbs

In normal adolescents, the hand that disturbs is often the hand of a monster or a deformed hand. In any case, it is never

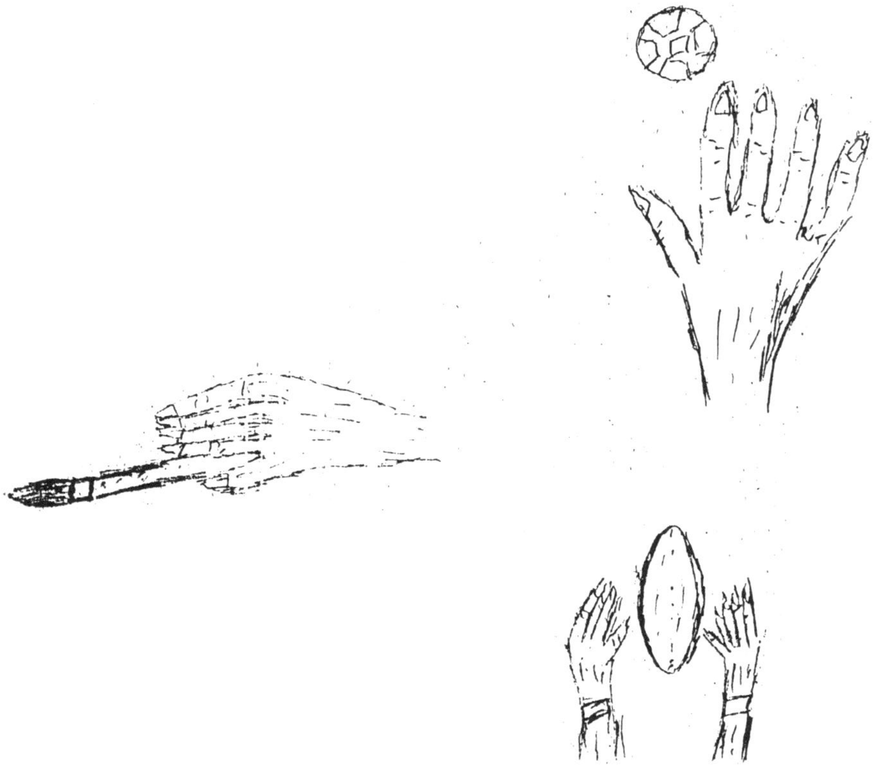

Figure 3.22
A Hand Drawing done by a 15-year-old sexual initiator.

their own hand. The monster may be the representation of the monster in themselves. The hand that disturbs should be included in testing of incarcerated adolescents. It is not described here because it was developed after I conducted testing in prisons.

The CHaD can help teenagers communicate their existential problems better and may help trigger dialogue. An adolescent, however, must never feel judged or compared to others. Adolescents are between two uncertain worlds, and the slightest push in either direction may aid or abet their identity.

THE CHaD IN THE ELDERLY

The case histories described in this section deal with elderly people placed in institutions for physical or mental handicaps. In contrast to other projective tests, the CHaD can respond to a certain number of questions such as the presence of genuine depression as compared to senility. Above all, it can be a means of reaching out to the elderly and facilitating relationships between patients and staff. Thus the CHaD has a therapeutic function. One of these functions is to enable the elderly to express themselves through drawing. This may give the elderly the awareness and the confidence that comes from realizing they can still produce something personal of value. This in a sense may obviate the vicious circle of emotional and physical dependence.

The CHaD and Dialogue: Therapeutic Value

The following vignettes illustrate how the CHaD can shed a different light on communication with individuals who apparently refuse to dialogue, or who exhibit confusion.

Mrs. D is 96 and permanently in a wheelchair. She is a lovely woman who is "all there" and like many people of her age hardly talks at all except to wish it were "all over." She wants to die. I ask her to draw her Childhood drawing. She responds skeptically, "How do you expect me to remember? That was ninety years ago."

It is the day after Bastille Day, French Independence Day, and Mrs. D draws a large tricolor flag. All of a sudden she remembers that when she was a little girl, she drew a duck flapping his wings to fly away off the lake in the Boulogne woods. She draws a ducklike figure in the corner of her sheet. Then Mrs. D tells me a series of anecdotes about this time in her life in a parochial school. Overcome by her memories, she says to me, "You make me laugh and remember."

From this day on, Mrs. D dialogues better with the staff, who cease to perceive her as an old complaining lady but rather see her as someone with stories to tell. Mrs. D can finally talk about something other than death.

Mrs. Des is 98. Forever smiling, the staff consider her to be senile and hence she is somewhat ignored. I ask her to draw her childhood drawing and she scribbles a few lines and says she is from the Limousine area of France. She tells me she went to school in galoshes and proceeds to describe a number of scenes from her childhood in a fairly mechanical way. As she is telling me about her childhood a nurse comes in who is also from this same part of France. The nurse suddenly feels some solidarity with this old impaired woman and they start to exchange memories.

In most instances, it only takes a little effort to effect vast improvement between elderly patients and the staff. Elderly patients are often viewed with distaste by the staff because they cannot get out of their spiral of complaints about their discomfort.

The elderly may put up some resistance at the start of the CHaD. They are afraid they will no longer be able to complete the task. They feel so dependent that they believe they cannot do anything by themselves. They constantly denigrate themselves. Therefore, they are surprised and amazed to discover they can produce artwork of their own. Many want to keep their drawings, and what I tend to do is to ask them to make a copy of the original to hang on their walls or night tables, *to remind them that they are still capable of something.* These childhood drawings can be graphically impoverished but full of hope. One elderly lady was so surprised she could draw a chair that every time she saw me in the hospital she asked if she could draw another chair "to show her son." This perserverance as regards repetitive actions is a sign of deterioration but it also shows pride in waiting for her son to come, a feeling she had almost ceased to have.

Thus, the childhood drawing is a powerful means of accessing the emotional universe of the elderly, a part of their beings that is often "forgotten" or closeted.

Both the hand drawing and the hand that disturbs provide more specific information on self image and relationships in the here and now. The CHaD can be used successfully even with the apparently very senile (see case of Mrs. P: "Dementia or Depression"). Although the hospital staff caring for Mrs. P was convinced that she was senile, the coherency of her statements on the CHaD and her understanding of the instructions (carried out in a way that did indeed represent her unfortunate reality) suggested depression much more than senility. This intense suffering that had taken on the mask of senility was thus revealed to the nursing staff. They were then in a position to improve their care of her.

The three CHaD drawings form a set of complementary information that sheds light on the mental state of the elderly. *Refusal to draw* is equally informative. A man approaching his 100th birthday said "Drawing is for others. They've got problems, not me." A 102-year-old woman refused to draw saying "I don't feel as able as I used to. I don't want to leave a deteriorated picture behind. I don't see very well any more, I broke my wrist recently, and my strokes would be wobbly." These refusals convey the wish to appear fragile to others. This woman is threatened by the idea of concretizing this fragility in a drawing (a threat to her own integrity). A very smart-looking woman with no sign of senility also refused to draw: the staff thought she was so curious and interested in political events that she would certainly live until the next presidential elections. She remained delighted to see me on the ward and would talk to me about her plans but she refused to be part of a psychological inquiry.

Another example of refusal is the case of a 99-year-old woman. Her pretext was that she couldn't see well any more. She wanted me to get the doctors to give her "the final shot." Because she didn't want to draw, I asked her to tell me what she would have drawn if she could have done so. Mrs. G described her childhood drawing to me, her age at the time, her past as a concert hall singer, her students, and came alive again. By the end of the discussion she was no longer talking about the final shot; instead she wanted to know when I could come back.

The CHaD thus enables the practitioner to reach out in a very personalized way to the elderly because it respects their desire to reveal themselves to whatever extent they wish. Some people are proud of their drawings, whereas others do not want to tarnish their image. All, however, manifest a desire to communicate and to show, despite appearances, that they are still capable beings, still alive, and able to leave their marks, the testimony of their lives.

The elderly appear to be seeking out death and begging to die with such insistence that one's first reaction is to get a doctor to comfort them. In fact, they are primarily expressing a dearth of communication and suffering linked to dependence. The psychologist's role is to create ties by making a request that enables the elderly to express their discomfort and to help them put their suffering into words.

The elderly should not be viewed as "immortals," and the subject of death and dying should not be taboo. The very old and suffering know that they are going to die and the psychologist is not there to stop them from talking about death and their perfectly warranted anxieties. Rather, the psychologist is there to help them name the unnameable, to speak of death. Once elderly persons are relieved of the burden of unspoken anxieties, they can once again think about life. Few staff members like to talk about death as a banal event, a universal fatality, affecting us all. Their attitude is perhaps related to the feeling that only the elderly can die. The idea of death is often cloaked or disguised, and it is helpful for the psychologist to bring it out into the open. The CHaD, because it elicits self-image, deals directly with the question of death. Patients stop talking about death or the "final shot" because the CHaD brings them back to their childhood when everything was still possible. Many patients hide behind monotone and superficial exteriors or have minds that wander, as though they wanted to escape reality.

The instructions to produce the childhood drawing snap them back into reality. Even when the drawing itself is hard to decipher, most subjects still understand the instructions.

This makes dialogue possible and helps provide the elderly with imaginal recollections they may be able to maintain for long periods of time. This gives them an additional dimension that facilitates their relationship to the staff.

The CHaD goes beyond complicated family relationships. It may reactivate the ability to identify, or it may enable individuals to represent themselves differently than through a collection of symptoms.

The CHaD and Senility

The CHaD, beyond its usefulness as an instigator of dialogue, can also be used to measure degree of senility. The CHaD may provide a better method of screening for senility than other tests, and may be more reliable. In particular, it helps differentiate senility from a form of depression with senile features.

The following case history shows how the CHaD can successfully screen for senility when there are no apparent signs of deterioration.

Mrs. C's Calligraphy

Mrs. C was born in June 1894 and was 96 when she took the CHaD. She seems clinically present and coherent. But when Mrs. C hears the instructions, she writes "childhood drawing she produced in her childhood" (figure 3.23). Curiously she writes "hand that disturbs" for the hand drawing (figure 3.24) and "hand" (figure 3.25) for the other task. To draw hands, she uses her own hands as a model. Instead of drawing however, she writes. For the hand that disturbs, she again uses her hand as a model and concentrates to "repre-

Figure 3.23
Calligraphy by Mrs. C. She writes, "childhood drawing she produced in her childhood."

Figure 3.24
Hand Drawing by Mrs. C. Strangely, she writes, "hand that disturbs."

Figure 3.25
Hand that Disturbs Drawing by Mrs. C. She writes, "draw a hand."

sent" it. Mrs. C is unaware that she is writing rather than drawing. Mrs. C understands the gist of the instructions and comments coherently on her "drawings": "It was a boat going down the Rhône River, I was born in Lyon, my father was the personal secretary to the governor of Lyon." If Mrs. C's paper had been concealed, I would have been convinced that she had drawn the scene. I term this type of written drawing calligraphy.

This patient is beginning to deteriorate, and the CHaD provides the first clinical evidence. There are no other visible signs of decline. Thus, the borderline between writing and drawing appears to be one indication of incipient senility.

Calligraphy is a common feature in senile patients, who are convinced that they are drawing. Since drawing is developmentally earlier than writing, it is somewhat striking to see that writing remains longer. A number of features in the CHaD drawings help determine the level of emotional or cognitive impairment. Most drawings in the very old are awkward, wobbly, and small. The significant signs of deterioration are:

- Forgetting purpose. The subject is unable to remember the meaning of the instructions.
- Use of calligraphy instead of drawing. Calligraphy can be a forerunner of Alzheimer's disease.

- Undecipherable drawings. This is a sign of the most severe impairment.

On the other hand, a discrepancy between a coherent CHaD and an apparent deterioration in the everyday life of an individual may be a sign of major depression. In this case, specific therapy can help. In contrast, the presence of calligraphy may be an early indicator of Alzheimer-type diseases.

DEMENTIA OR DEPRESSION?

Mrs. P is 89. She is an inward-directed woman, and her speech is incoherent. The nursing staff considers her to be extremely senile. She agrees to sit down to take the test. She speaks quickly and is hard to understand, but as soon as she hears the instructions, she musters her energy, draws, and comments in the following way.

The Childhood Drawing

"Little girl, I did something with my father. We made a little pig, that was fifty five years ago. I don't think I could do it now. We did like this. Each thing had a number." Mrs. P smiles and adds, "you know, I remember." She draws a small, unidentifiable animal in the corner of the sheet, which looks more like a cat with chicken feet, with a corkscrew tail (figure 3.26). She does not use color.

The Hand Drawing

"A hand? A kind of hand?" (ten seconds latency). "A hand with nails. We have five fingers, one, two, three, four, five.

Figure 3.26
Mrs. P's Childhood Drawing.

The fifth is the smallest, we'll give him something." Mrs. P. adds a small line. She draws a second hand: "One finger, two fingers, three, that makes five."

The hands are rectangles with points for fingers. The stroke is strong, but the drawings are rectified and unfinished. The hands are small and located at the top left of the sheet.

The Hand That Disturbs

This hand is similar in location and size to the hand drawings. The second hand appears to be lying down. "It's more difficult, the left hand: one finger, two fingers, a wrist. That's one more for you. I can't bend my wrist any more. I'll give you the arm, that will make one more for you."

Inquiry and Comments

The Childhood Drawing: My little pig has a corkscrew tail. I was it. It was a game I always lost and I went to the toilet and cried. I was a poor loser.

The Hand Drawing: They are mine; they aren't doing anything anymore.

The Hand That Disturbs: It's kaput. They don't want to be bothered, they don't want to work anymore.

Which hand do you prefer? "I prefer the hand that disturbs, the kaput one because it can't do anything anymore. I don't expect anything from people anymore, I want to go into the hole. I only think of dying. That's the most interesting thing in life."

Mrs. P shows no senility, and a diagnosis of depression is much more likely than Alzheimer's disease.

THE RAG DOLL

Miss R was born on September 1, 1900 and was 90 when administered the CHaD. She is a very distinguished-looking woman with her hair drawn back carefully into a bun. She has a bookshelf in her room. She reads a great deal and is in charge of the patients' library. She is very interested in meeting me and is quite happy to have a chance to talk to someone.

The Childhood Drawing

Miss R draws a person with its arms outstretched, with no face, dressed in a kind of blue coat (figure 2.1). The hands and feet are incomplete. Despite its sparseness, the drawing is pretty and Miss R takes her time and draws with care. "A doll. It's a little messed up." Miss R spontaneously asks if she can use color. "There, that's lovely!" (figure 2.1).

The Hand Drawing

"My father was an engineer. I came from a good family." Miss R draws two tiny, poorly constructed hands, in the lower part of the sheet. She lightly sketches two rectangular wrists topped with points.

The Hand That Disturbs

"You said someone I don't like. Really I don't know. (15 sec. latency). "I'll draw an ordinary hand." Miss R draws a hand similar to the preceding ones.

Inquiry and Comments

The Childhood Drawing: "I was the third girl and my mother wanted a boy. I had a doll; when I turned 13 my mother forced me to take it to the Children's Hospital. Give that to children! I took care of it. Even now it hurts. I wouldn't have been sadder if I had had to give up my own child."

The Hand Drawing: "They are my hands, I use them to knit."

The Hand That Disturbs: "A patient who said she wouldn't shake my hand any more."

There was high coherency between drawings and comments. Miss R was in the here-and-now, and her relationships to others emerge clearly. There is no pathology in this elderly lady but 80 years later the event which was to leave permanent marks on this woman was still apparent. Miss R never had (or couldn't have) children. Was this because she lost her first child, her rag doll?

THE CHaD IN NORMAL SUBJECTS

THE BLACK MOTHER

E is about 40.

The Childhood Drawing

E quickly recalls her childhood drawing. She says she thinks about it often. The drawing is of a black woman dressed in traditional African clothing who is carrying her baby wrapped on her back (figure 3.27). This beautiful African woman is making a meal by pounding grain, in a genuine African setting. The decor is simple but harmonious. The colors are clear pastels.

The Hand Drawing

E draws three average-sized hands (figure 3.28). The hands are arranged vertically on the sheet in a harmonious fashion. The first hand on the top is the profile of a right hand with a long wrist (no closure line). The second hand, underneath the first, shows the back of a left hand, with prominent nails and knuckles. The fingers are close together. The third hand is a right hand, palm up. Four fingers cover the palm. The thumb, fairly large, sticks up.

The Hand That Disturbs

E draws a vertical left hand, palm down (figure 3.29). The thumb cannot be seen. The index and middle finger make a V, and the remaining two fingers are bent at the knuckle. There are some rectifications.

Inquiry and Comments

E is white and has never lived in or been to Africa. This childhood drawing seems a little dreamlike, a distant fantasy. The child in the drawing is very close to the mother, and in fact E draws the close relationship she longed for but never had with her own mother. The drawing presents the

Figure 3.27
Black mother's Childhood Drawing.

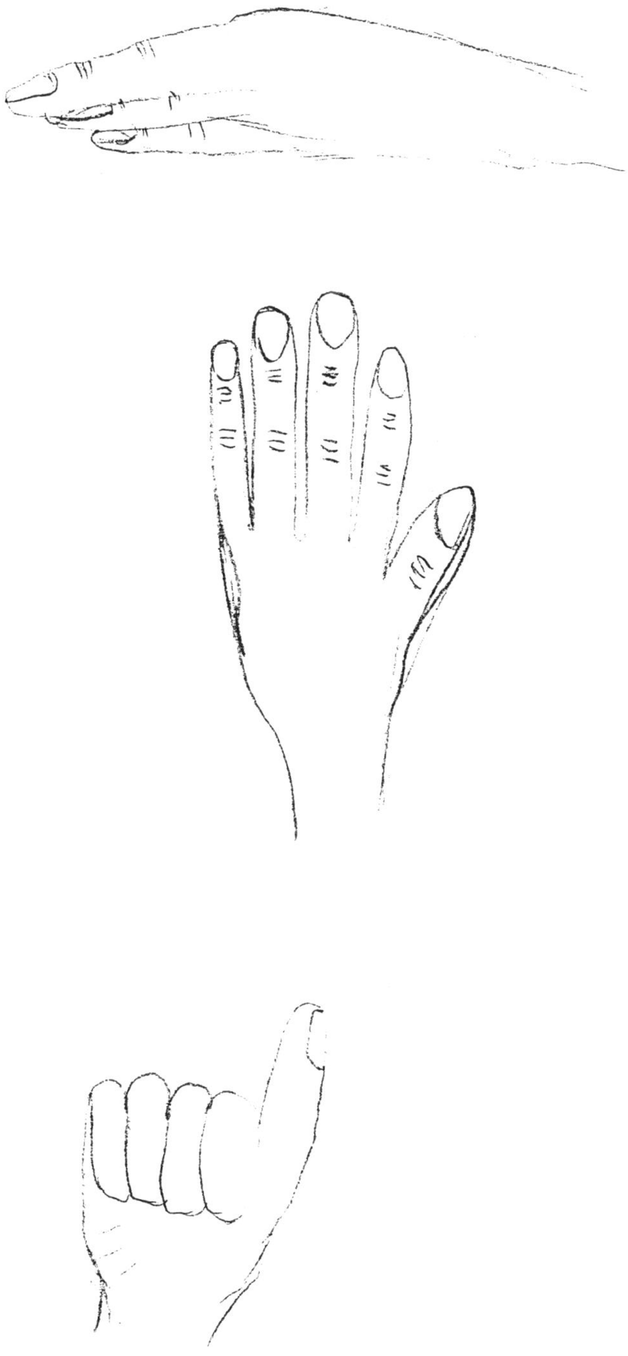

Figure 3.28
Black mother's Hand Drawing.

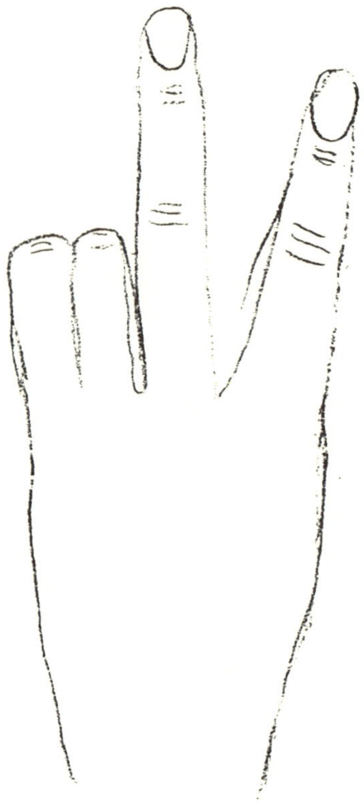

Figure 3.29
Black mother's Hand that Disturbs Drawing.

contrary of this poor mother-daughter relationship by situating different-skin protagonists in a faraway country. The real mother-child relationship is repressed by depicting this happy mother-infant dyad.

CHaD drawings that are made with extreme care and beauty tend to be cues to the poor relationship of examinees to the figure they depict. During the inquiry E indicates that her relationship with her mother is still difficult. E discovered the meaning of her childhood drawing for the first time during the inquiry. She was unaware that her drawing had such painful sources.

The Hand Drawing: The set of three hands is harmoniously distributed on the page. The overall stroke is clean, although some of the lines are hesitant. The use of nails and knuckles is indicative of concern with outward appearance. But the fingers tightly concealing the palm indicate high self-control, the need to filter communication and not to show emotions. The fact that E drew three hands in three different positions shows that she is unsure of herself and that she reveals little of herself. Her self-doubt may stem from her poor relationship with her mother.

The Hand That Disturbs: "It's a hand that is making the V for victory," says E. "It's a hand that disturbs because it is a hand that shows something and is showing off." E hates all forms of exhibitionism and finds any show of emotion distasteful. The hand that disturbs is a recapitulation of the timid child who shifted her conflicts to a distant continent and today prefers not to say what she really thinks, even when this makes her appear shy or not straightforward.

In a sense, the more distant the setting, the closer the conflict. An idyllic landscape expresses conflict with the real world. The drawing becomes an imaginary world, a mental construct that enables E to flee reality.

THE TRAIN DRIVER

H is about 40, and seems somewhat shy. He rapidly recalls his childhood drawing.

The Childhood Drawing

H draws a bouquet of different colored flowers in a vase on a round table (figure 3.30).

The Hand Drawing

H draws two large hands, one palm up and the other palm down (figure 3.31). The hands are anatomical and realistic. There is a space between each finger. What is striking about these hands is the contrast between their well-structured dimensions and the impression of strength they produce, and the high number of small strokes and lines on the surface of the hands.

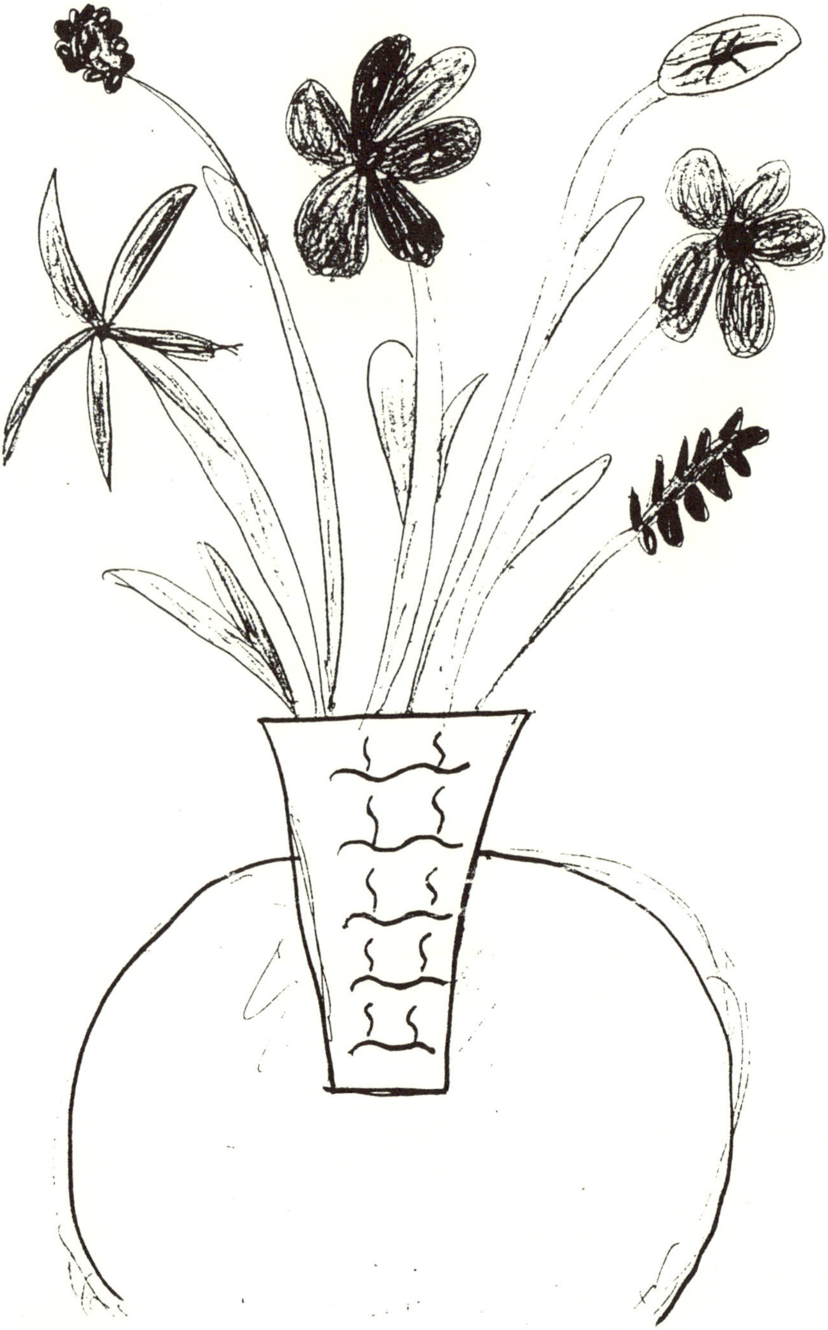

Figure 3.30
Train driver's Childhood Drawing.

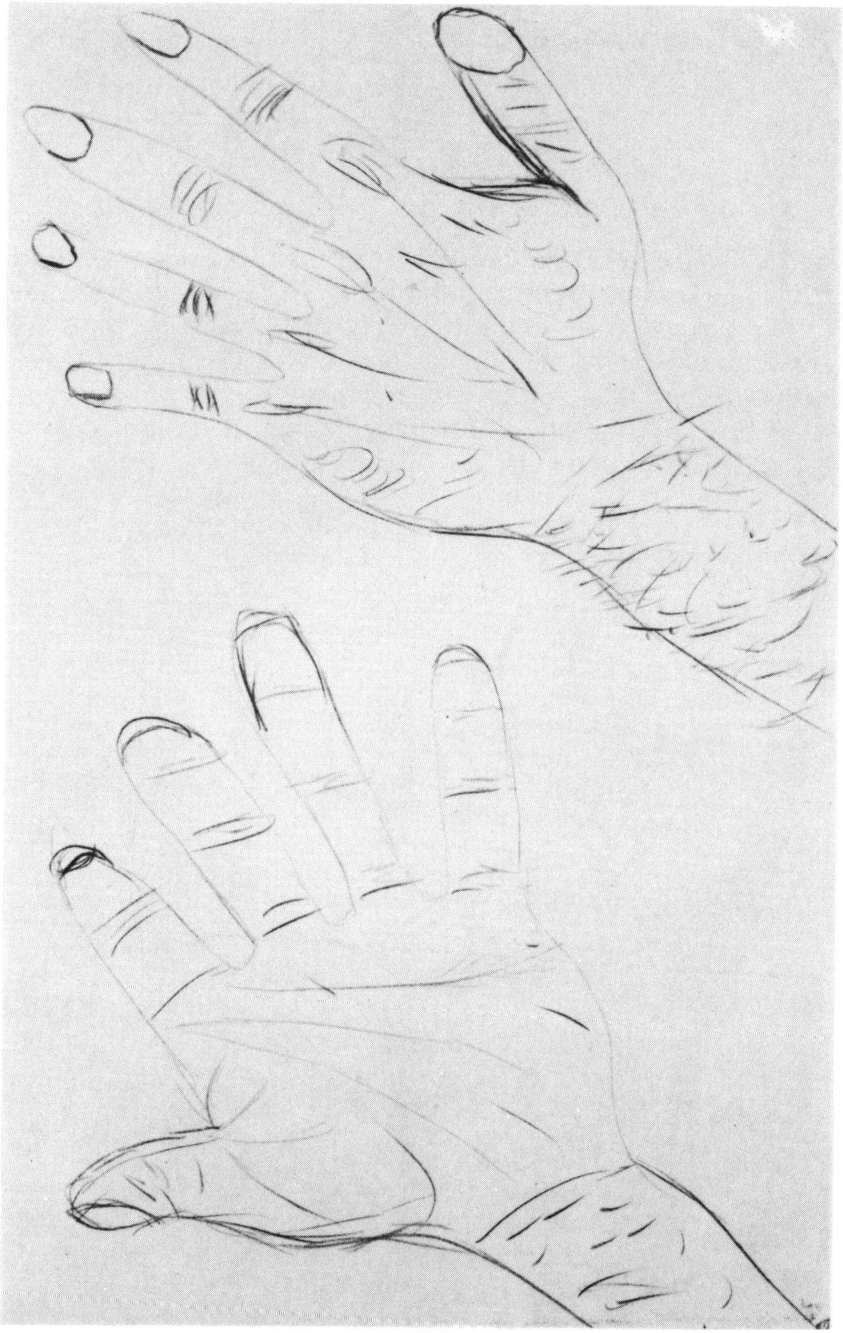

Figure 3.31
Train driver's Hand Drawing.

The Hand That Disturbs

H draws a large hand with peculiar crooked fingers (figure 3.32).

Inquiry and Comments

The Childhood Drawing: The flowers reflect H's sensitivity. H always had to pretend to be "tough." He was the younger of two boys and his feminine tendencies were perhaps unconsciously encouraged by his mother. However, the flowers which reflect this sensitivity are firmly set in an enclosed vase and placed on a table, symbolizing another closed (though incomplete) circle.

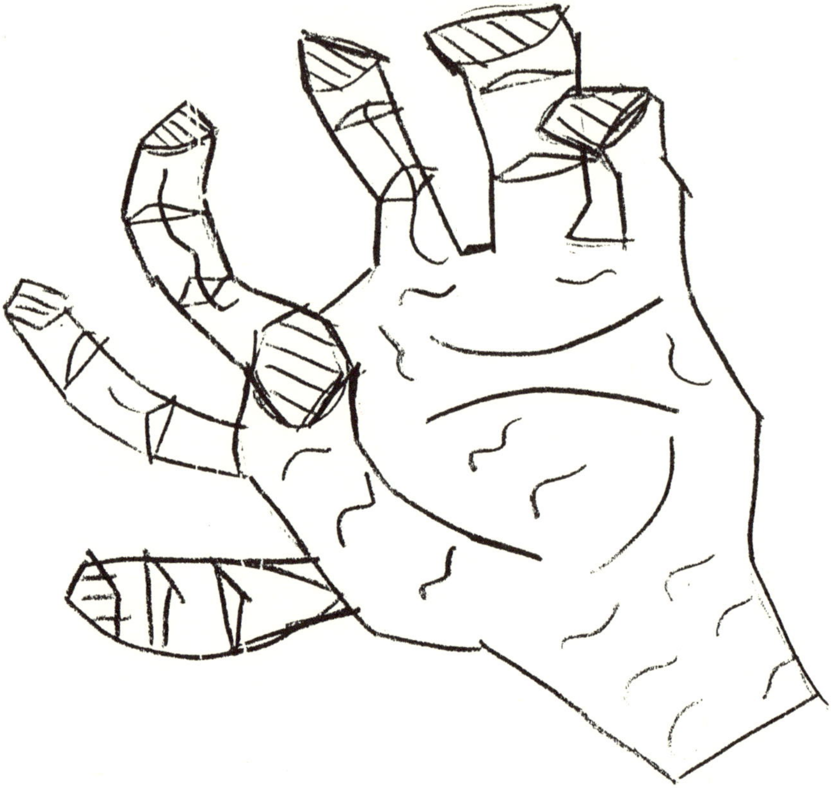

Figure 3.32
Train driver's Hand that Disturbs Drawing.

The Hand Drawing: H has no trouble communicating with others. However, the large number of strokes, lines, and hairs on the hands show that this self-confidence has been examined consciously and is controlled. The presence of hair may suggest a feeling of inferiority. H is short, and he may compensate for his size by emphasizing masculine characteristics.

The number of lines also reflects anxiety and the lines on the palm are suggestive of emotional trauma: H is divorced and has just left his girlfriend. These traits, associated with an open palm, indicate that this anxiety is controlled. H is a train driver and his hands are comparable to the ones made by a pilot. Both hands reflect strength and sensitivity and may suggest the demands of the profession.

The Hand That Disturbs: The hand does not belong to H. He states that the hand is "deformed" and "sick," being in pieces as though it had gone "through the meat grinder." The hand frightens him. He must be afraid of it personally and professionally because of the risk of (occupational) incapacitation. There are as many lines and strokes on the hand that disturbs as on the hand drawing. This may imply that H's anxiety is linked primarily to a fear of impotence.

THE SAILBOAT

F is in her thirties, and is happy to draw.

The Childhood Drawing

The drawing is a reproduction of the seascape that F's parents had in their living room (figure 3.33). The picture fascinated her, and she enjoyed copying the two sailboats sailing on the calm blue water.

The Hand Drawing

F produces a harmonious drawing of two large hands (figure 3.34). There is an attempt at artistry. There are spaces between the fingers of the hand on the right side of the page. The hand on the left is in profile, and the fingers are curved together.

Figure 3.33
F's Childhood Drawing.

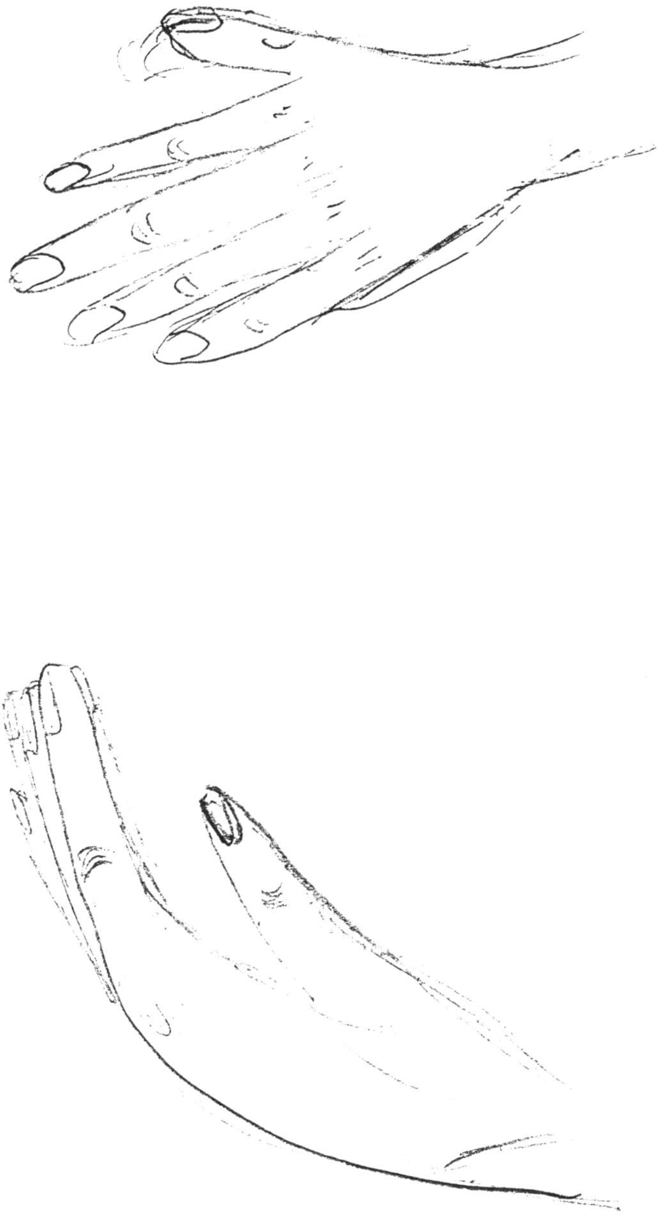

Figure 3.34
F's Hand Drawing.

The Hand That Disturbs

F draws a "witch's" hand, with long, crooked fingers and pointed nails (figure 3.35).

Inquiry and Comments

The Childhood Drawing: The overall composition is harmonious. It suggests that her childhood must have been a happy one. The choice of a childhood drawing is often dictated by an adult wish. Children tend to produce drawings that adults like the most, and the drawing can be an

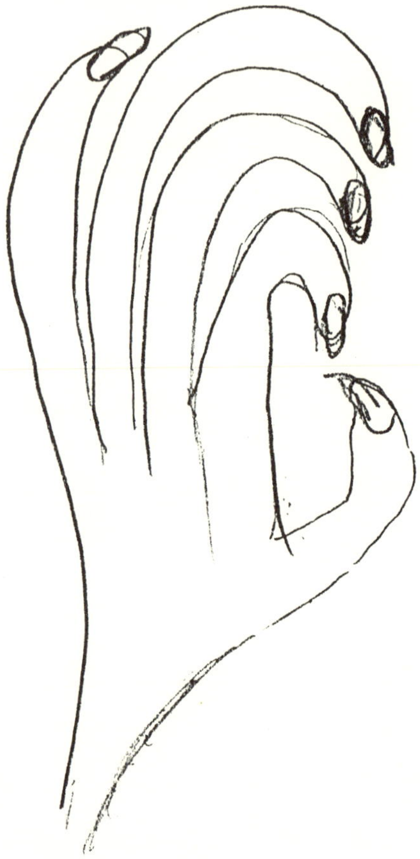

Figure 3.35
F's Hand that Disturbs Drawing.

"ideal" that provides a reassuring image of the family circle. Here the boats rocking on the waves are reassuring and soothing.

The Hand Drawing: The distance separating each finger is identical for the hand on the right. F must not reveal much of herself and probably only communicates on a superficial level with the people around her. The impression of harmony in the hands is due to a large extent to the artist's need to protect her outward appearance, here through efforts at an artistic presentation.

The Hand That Disturbs: The hand does not belong to F. The circle formed by the thumb and index finger may suggest sexual dissatisfaction. F's deepest tendencies are revealed in the hand that disturbs. The blackened nails suggest depression. Thus, even in this normal individual, conflicts leave traces.

THE CARTOON

G is 23 and volunteers to take the CHaD.

The Childhood Drawing

G draws a large figure that looks like a character from a comic book: a crosseyed comic book figure with big ears and a clown's mouth (figure 3.36). He makes abundant use of color. G is Italian, and the choice in particular of red, green, and white may represent his background. The colors of the Italian flag are red, green, white.

The hands have pointed nails and are covered with brown strokes. The lower abdomen has blue stripes and a yellow star in the center. A brown belt with vertical stripes separates chest and abdomen. In the ears, there are brown strokes that look somewhat like question marks. The figure is wearing a banana-hat.

The figure has a red standup collar. It has an enormous capital letter script G on his chest, corresponding to G's first name. G signs the picture with a red script "G" on the right-hand side of the sheet.

Figure 3.36
G's Childhood Drawing.

The Hand Drawing

G makes two large hands with fine strokes (figure 3.37). One hand is seen palm down, and the other is palm up. The hand on the left-hand side looks a little like a glove and is cut off by black slanted lines at the wrist. The ring finger of the palm-up figure is thinner at the base and reworked. Palm lines and age lines appear on the palm.

The Hand That Disturbs

G draws a fleshy hand (figure 3.38). The index finger is in the nose of a large face drawn in profile. The nose is the largest part of the face and is depicted as a cone. Both nostrils are shown on the same side of the nose. The mouth is shut and the eye is a slit. The head is not shown because the face reaches the top of the sheet at eye level. There is a bracelet shape on the wrist. The nails are colored black.

Inquiry

The Childhood Drawing: G says that the comic strip figure is a drawing he made often when he was a teenager. Who is the person? It is clearly a male figure who could be his father or perhaps G himself. The capital "G" on the T-shirt clearly reflects G's first name. The figure denigrates the person it represents through caricature, and seems to suggest that G is making fun of or devaluing himself. G had a happy childhood but lacked self confidence. He felt dominated by an all-powerful father. This caricature represents himself as much as it represents his father.

The Hand Drawing: The number of hands (two) and their size could suggest a positive self-image. But these positive elements are contradicted by the tiny lines, the light stroke, and the scribbles (in the palm). G "ruined" the ring finger, as though this finger, the symbol of union, represented an obstacle to the overall picture. In contrast, G seems to have no trouble depicting the other fingers. In the hand on the right, which looks like a right hand, the lines in the palm look like the lines for a left hand as though G confused left and right when dealing with one kind of symbolism: marriage.

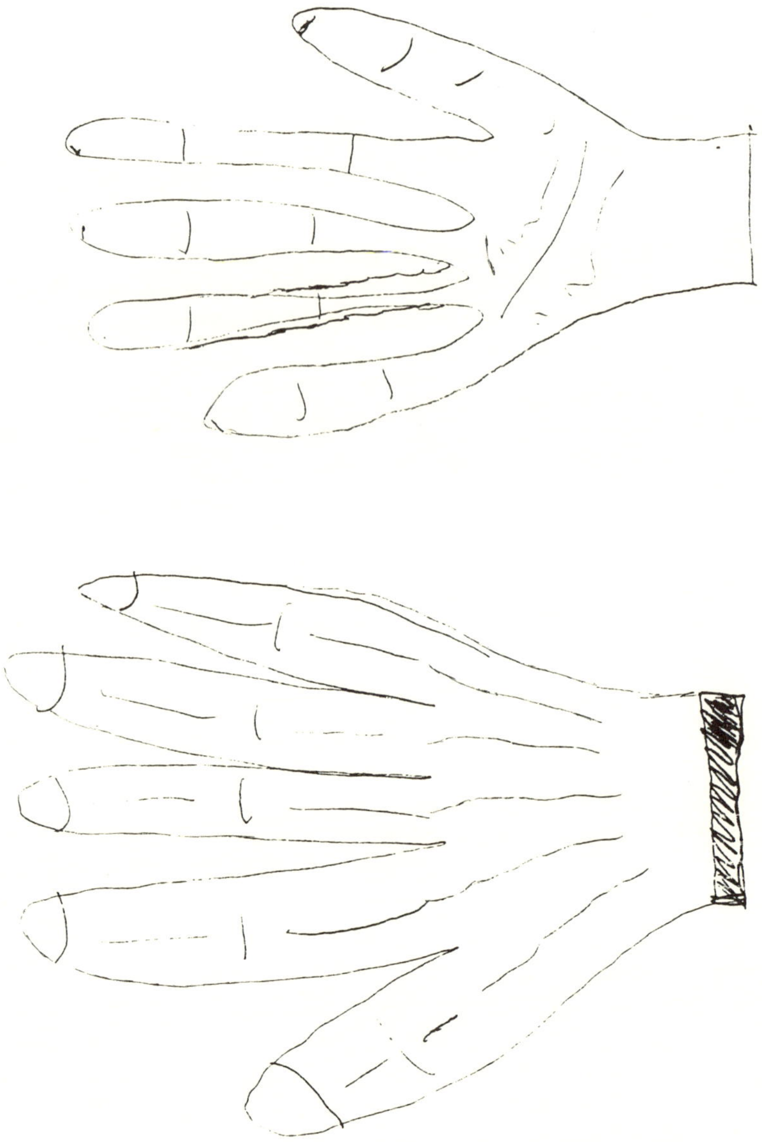

Figure 3.37
G's Hand Drawing.

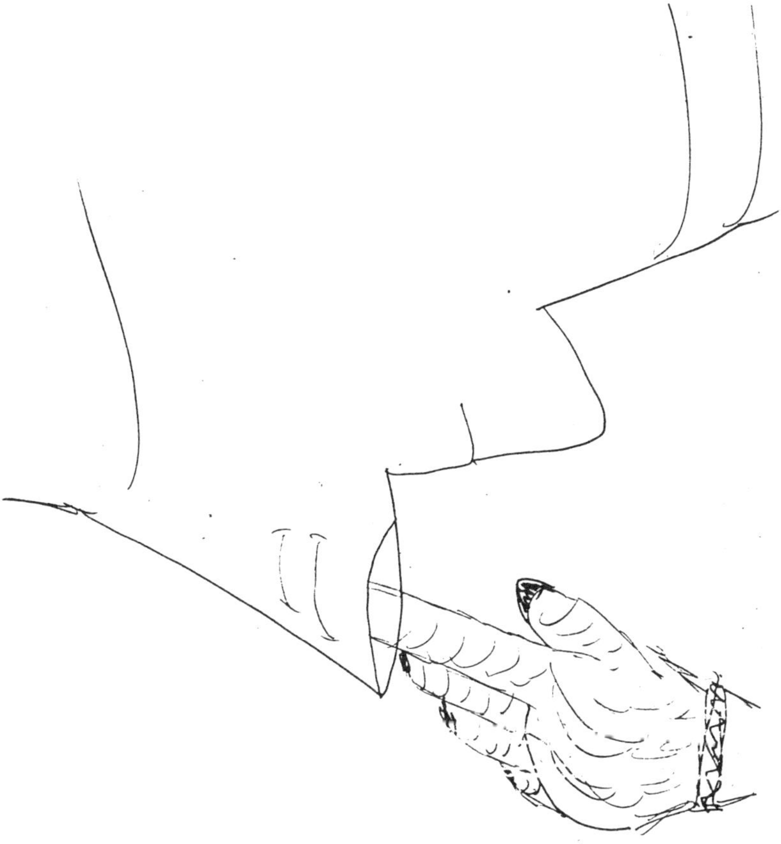

Figure 3.38
G's Hand that Disturbs Drawing.

The Hand That Disturbs: G has no trouble drawing the hand that disturbs; he states it is a "facade," a societal hand: "I hate people that put their fingers in their noses." Beyond good manners, a more basic issue is involved — penetration. G says he suffers from premature ejaculation and lost all self confidence beginning in adolescence.

Thus hidden in this drawing, which G meant to be entertaining, lies sexual anxiety. The cut-off wrist may express the guilt linked to masturbation. The hand that disturbs looks similar to the hands in the childhood drawing, as though the hands were there to remind us that the root cause of the sexual problem was already present in the childhood drawing. The crisscrossed strokes in the face and the stroke used "below the belt" are identical and reveal G's sexual problems.

THE CHaD IN PATIENTS IN PSYCHIATRIC WARDS

THE DEVIL

Z, a woman in her 30s, is tall and thin. She is wearing a somewhat dirty pair of jeans and a sweater with holes in it. Z has been interned in a psychiatric ward because she is "mute, in a stupor, and in a severe catatonic state."

Once hospitalized Z ceases to be mute and makes delirious statements such as she is the devil and is afraid of hurting others with her words, or that her three children aged 12, 10 and 7 are locked up in a hospital room.

The Childhood Drawing

Z is somewhat distrustful, and the idea of making a drawing is apparently unpleasant to her. She is reserved and fearful of encountering another member of the hospital staff, in particular a psychologist. But when she hears the instructions, she seems more confident. As though the instructions had reassured her, Z makes a tiny drawing in the upper left-hand portion of the page (figure 3.39). In fact, Z apparently forgets the instructions and draws her own

Figure 3.39
Z's Childhood Drawing.

house, first in pencil and then in red, brown, and green crayon. After she finishes the house she adds a vegetable garden with "carrots and leeks." The sadness of the house drawing stems from the grey and white fence around the garden. The alignment of vegetables makes them look like tombstones. There is a sharp contrast between the brightly colored house in red and brown with its green path and the grey, sad garden.

The Hand Drawing

Z draws two tiny hands with light strokes in the upper left-hand corner of the page (figure 3.40). Z says they are children's hands, or a puppet's hands. The left hand has six fingers. The lines are wavering. The wrist is open.

Figure 3.40
Z's Hand Drawing.

The Hand That Disturbs

Z immediately draws a tiny hand with claws (figure 3.41). The hand resembles a devil's hand, reflecting Z's major preoccupation. The stroke is uniform. The nails are blackened. Although it has claws, the hand is not deformed.

Inquiry and Comments

The Childhood Drawing: There is no regression, in terms of either artwork (the picture is adultlike) or commentary, since Z states it is the house she lives in now. We know, however, from her case history that she left her family home in Brittany at a very early age to raise sheep in a town in the south of France. Despite this confusion, the drawing served as a mediator and triggered dialogue since Z began to talk after making this drawing.

Z places great emphasis on the garden where vegetables are growing. The issue is food, and Z is anorexic. The fact that she draws a garden whose shape and color suggest death leads directly to the core of Z's problems. The two vegetables mentioned by Z (carrots and leeks) are similar in that the edible part is also the buried part. The garden is somewhat like an iceberg: the part underground is more important because it is edible, and what Z depicts is an orderly surface as though everything related to food had to be hidden, buried, aligned, and controlled and look like a cemetery.

The Hand Drawing: Z says the hands belong to a child or to a puppet. Z may be attempting to detract power from the hands, since children's hands are generally not dangerous, and puppets' hands are lifeless. Z is afraid to draw her own

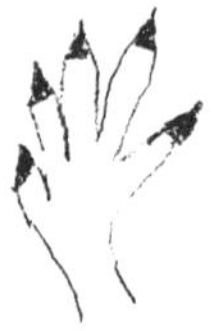

Figure 3.41
Z's Hand that Disturbs Drawing.

hands, because she does not want to disclose her own body image.

The Hand That Disturbs: Z does not speak when I ask her who the hand belongs to. She appears to be paralyzed; the hands with claws on the sheet seem to terrify her. This reaction helps explain her attempts to distance herself from hands. In her mind, the hand that disturbs is her own hand, a dangerous one that can scratch, or hurt.

As in other psychotic patients, the hand belongs to the patient. Z is unable to distance herself from her "devil's" hand. Regression, normally observed for the childhood drawing, took place here in the hand that disturbs. Although Z is unable to comment on this hand, it is clearly related to her delirium and to a theme that goes back to her childhood.

POOR DOG

This case concerns a 43-year-old man who killed his dog in a fit of madness by stabbing it to death, and wounded his girlfriend in the same manner.

The Childhood Drawing

The patient states immediately that his mother asked him to draw the weather in the area where they lived every day, and the sunrise and sunset. *"My mother made me do that, she didn't understand that it was useless, it's always nice on the Côte d'Azur. I had been thinking about how they had raised me wrong in the days just before the scene. I was a boy who always wanted to please his mother. I made the drawing in india ink, I added colors. My mother put the drawing up on the wall. I made the sky blue because it was blue. I didn't like it. I don't have a happy memory of it. I didn't do well in the local school because of that. In the 6th form I made a drawing of a map and the number of meters, I don't know whether it was a map for a battle but it was done in india ink. I was a perfectionist, if there was a little spot I erased it with the eraser and I ended up making holes so I started another one on another sheet."*

Then, after a long period of latency, the patient made a spot with the pencil, drew a zig-zag over it without lifting the pencil and tried to erase and tore the paper while crumpling it. Then he took another sheet, squared it off by drawing 24 small rectangles: he drew suns in three rectangles (circles with needles like a sea urchin), two of which were in pencil and colored yellow, in a solid blue sky (figure 3.42)

The Hand Drawing

The patient says, "They aren't very nice, they are not very open, they look like a cartoon. Puppet hands. Shall I do the shirt?"

The patient draws two small ill-structured hands, with wrists cleanly cut off by the buttoned cuff of a shirt (3.43). Both hands are reaching toward a type of parallelogram with a hole pierced through it. One hand, whose fingers are together, is colored grey and is hence opaque. The stroke is saw-toothed. The second hand has the fingers spread apart in the form of a bouquet of flowers, with no embellishments. In both cases, the strokes do not overlap, giving the hands a sad and unfinished look.

The Hand That Disturbs

The patient's first reaction is to say, "And if there isn't one?" He then draws two hands: the hands are tiny, shapeless, and only have three fingers (figure 3.44). They are shaded in with pencil and look like they have been colored black. "Maybe with two fingers," he adds (he adds two fingers, one over the other); "like that, yes, that bothers me; often it's when something is missing, there, there are two fingers. I really feel ill at ease when something doesn't have a leg or a finger, it's castration anxiety."

He then adds two fingers, one on top of the other on the second hand.

Interview

The Childhood Drawing: G states that he was 8 when he drew for purposes of getting good grades and pleasing his mother. When he got his high school diploma, it was published in the local newspaper and his mother cut the article

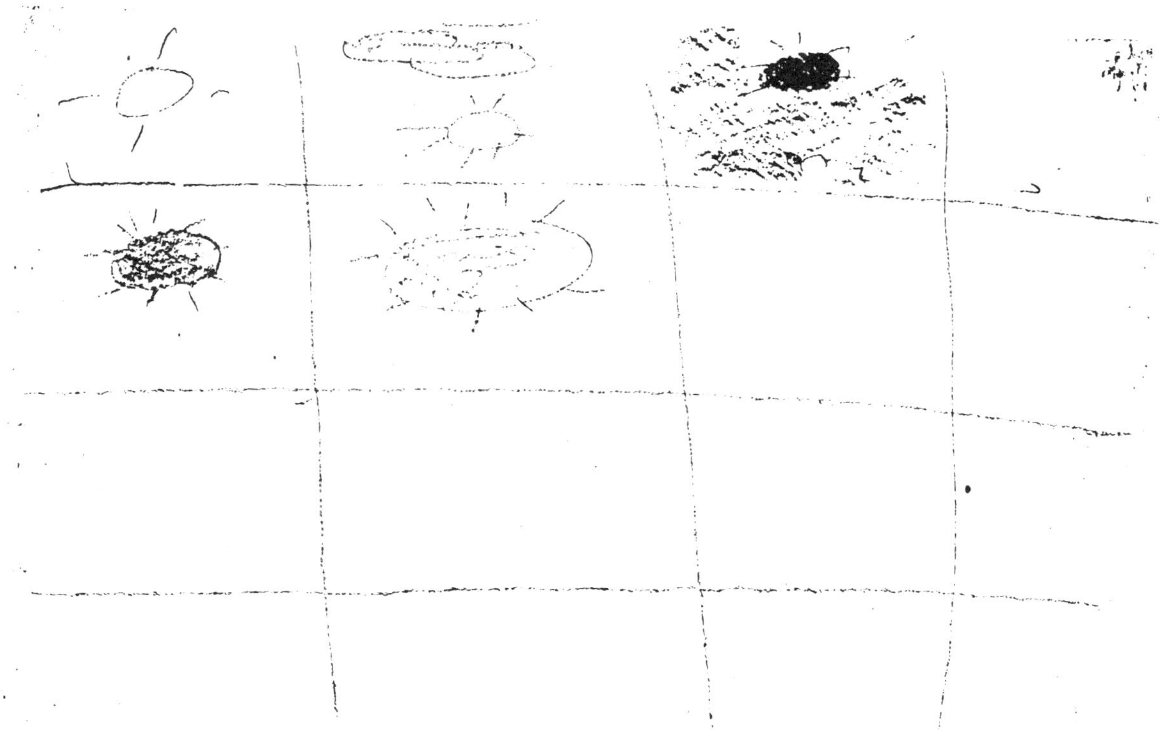

Figure 3.42
The 43-year-old dog killer's Childhood Drawing.

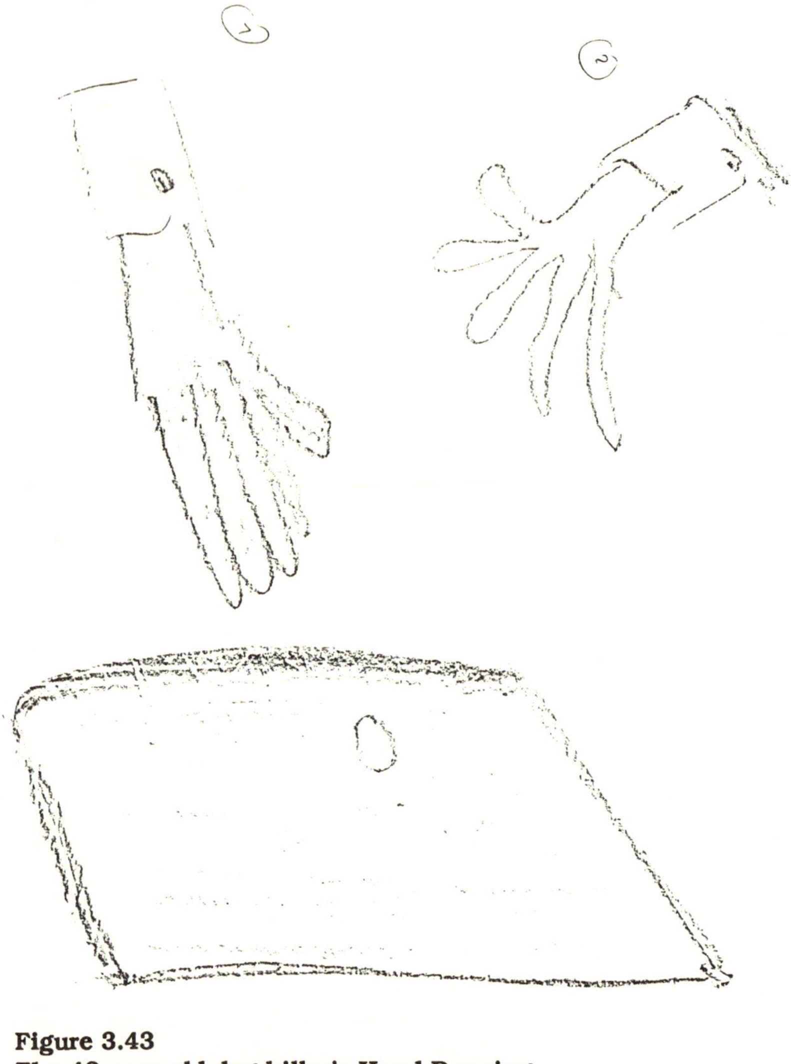

Figure 3.43
The 43-year-old dog killer's Hand Drawing.

Figure 3.44
The 43-year-old dog killer's Hand that Disturbs Drawing.

out. When he became a postmaster, he was sorry that Paris didn't have a newspaper to publish it like the one on the Côte d'Azur.

G says that he cried twice in his life. Once, he shed two tears the night his aunt died and the second time in prison because of his dog's death. His aunt was his father's sister. His father died when he was 8, and he was raised by his father's sister, a spinster who had been engaged before 1914 to a man who died in the first world war. She was a nurse. "It was a problem of the first world war. My aunt lived with my parents." As regards his father, G says, "He was someone with no ambition who had no schooling despite the opportunities . . . " He adds, "Naturally my father was a Nazi leader" and combines his father, mother, and girlfriend in his comments. G adds that he hated his parents: "They weren't even worth the price of the bullets to kill them."

He cried for the first time when his aunt died, although he was known to have hit this same aunt with electric wires in the past. She had complained about it and asked him to stop. He didn't tell anyone about it. This took place when she started to go senile, when he was about 13.

G then talks about how he killed flies in the sun by burning them with a magnifying glass. He built a sophisticated prison with a roll of scotch tape, and he explains how he made the roll waterproof. He put the fly in, added water, and cooked the whole thing.

The second time he cried, as he said, was in prison, in memory of his dog. He called his dog "son." G said he wanted to have a child with his girlfriend but that he thought children were dirty and that you always had to wash them.

G talked about his strong feelings when he saw the dog's genitals and that he had an erection. He also talked about his admiration for this dog the first time the dog urinated by lifting a leg. Then G talked about "his father, he was violent."

"In the beginning I was violent with my dog because he ate his dog-do. I read a book about dogs that said that dogs that had undergone violence when they were "children" acted like that." After reading this book G stopped hitting his dog and the dog stopped eating his excrement.

The Hand Drawing: When asked, "What are the hands doing," he answered: "Not really hands that are touching. They are funny. The open hand is getting ready to grab something, there might just be a door."

The Hand That Disturbs: "It's not the hand of anyone in particular, but rather the hand of a young person, a young boy. I could have turned out like that too, the V for victory it's not that I don't like it, I think it's ridiculous, people who do that."

The first childhood drawing is a drawing executed under orders (or commissioned by his mother). G says he was 8 when he made the drawing (again his age when his father died). This also corresponds to the period when he lived with his aunt.

The second period, at about the age of 13, was when his aunt died. He apparently terrorized this aunt who couldn't stand "stains." He crumples and tears up his drawings and says he is a "perfectionist." This is the period when he was interested in cooked flies. Each of these two childhood drawings reveals major periods in G's life: two deaths, the father, and the aunt whom he had been entrusted to.

G can claim he was a perfectionist, and in fact he appears not to have allowed himself to "ruin" or "spot" or "go outside the line," that is, to take any initiatives that were not approved by his mother. His response was to crumple and to tear and to throw away, in other words, to get rid of what did not correspond to his idea of what he or his mother would think or do. He is extremely disappointed that his mother cannot read about his promotions in the local newspaper, now that he is "anonymous" in a big city. When he was no longer controlled, he may have begun destroying and cutting up. That is what he did with his dog and girlfriend.

The fact that the first drawings are dated suggests that his disorders can be traced back to the age of 8 when his father died. His father's death was a major event in G's life, when he started to hit his aunt and catch flies. In a certain way he will attack all innocent beings whom he considers to be weaker than he is.

The hand drawing depicts "cartoon" hands, that is non-human, lifeless hands. Given that the hand drawing is a projection of the self, a representation of body image, it is likely that G projects into the inanimate, since he is incapable of representing a living part of himself. The instruction to "draw hands" does not prompt him to draw his own hands, which he does not use as a model. He places them at a distance by giving them a status of non-human object.

In the hand that disturbs drawing, G produces a *human* hand. It is not his own hand, and he does not appropriate it, which may suggest that there is no reason to deduce a psychosis. However, the contrast between the hand that disturbs (human and animate) and the hand drawing (self-image) of puppet, nonhuman hands is striking. It reveals that antagonism in G. When he heard the word "disturb," he immediately reacted by saying "It doesn't" and then added "It's not the hand of anyone in particular." This time G really heard the word "hand," which he gradually associated with some human being because he specified that it was a young person. Then he drew a "V for victory and people who do that."

G commented a great deal before, during, and after drawing. The stories he told are closer to confused digressions than to the structured comments appropriate to the instructions.

G narrated his acts of violence with no feelings of regret and mixed up stories of the people around him in a monotone voice. The only character that has life is his dog, whom he did not give "a dog's life" because he called him "son" and "child."

What is striking is the discrepancy between the violence of his acts and the lack of expressivity of violence in his comments (which he narrates more than he lives) in the three drawings. The only color used in the hand drawings is blackening, which, however, was reinforced. This may be a sign of insistence. To produce black G had to press hard on the pencil.

The CHaD served to reveal the psychotic and violent structure of the subject by presenting a violent subject (the hands are blackened and devitalized) when G talks about the hand drawing as "belonging to a person in a cartoon." This reveals the ambiguity of repetition of violence. G tells us about his violent father. In the few cases I have observed of particularly violent parents, with threats of knifings or being shot with a revolver, the children have a propensity for tearing up their drawings or cutting them up with scissors. G, for his part, tears and crumples up his childhood drawing.

The CHaD suggests that G's apraxia does not stem entirely from a psychotic disorder since children who have experienced violence draw hands that *touch or grasp.* Note, too, that apraxia is common in situations of emotional infantilism and perpetuates the situation of dependency and a refusal to grow up, which lead us back to G's comments that he only drew to please his mother. However, the opposition in G appears to play out the possibility to act and to be acted on. The hands that touch and grasp are lifeless. In other words, an image unknown to him is acting in his place.

Bear in mind that in the hand that disturbs drawing, the hand is a child's but is someone else's hand, yet still a child's. A comparison of the comments in the interview on the childhood drawing with what G.'s hands could do when he was a child, suggests that G's hands seem to project into the future, and are not as inoffensive or innocent as they may seem.

The CHaD enabled the subject to "talk himself out" in a short period of time with no real therapeutic help. The CHaD added a more "human" dimension to testing since the subject left asking the psychologist for advice as though he had sufficiently revealed himself for a specialist (the psychologist) to give him informed advice. "Do you think my girlfriend will want to see me again?" Poor dog.

DANIELLE—NO LIMITS

Danielle is 32 years old, and has been placed in a psychiatric ward for schizophrenia. She is cute, looks very young, and is very stylish and casual. During the short interview I had with her before I asked her to draw, she immediately invited me into her private universe and talked to me about "Frederic" as though I knew him well and understood her references to him.

The Childhood Drawing

Danielle responds quickly to the instructions. She draws a house (figure 3.45) and then asks for another sheet of paper that she uses to draw a figure. A house is a commonplace theme, a house with a great deal of color. The construction, however, is striking: the edges of the sheet are the walls. The roof blends into the sky. This overly well-aligned house with its geometric openings gives an impression of rigidity.

This rigidity is even more apparent in the parting of the curtains in the windows and the round center window which exhibit both striking symmetry and stereotypicality.

She then draws a figure with a round face and a red, pointed hat. The figure was first sketched in pencil, and the shirt and shorts were then drawn over in blue. She colors the eyes over in green. The eyes seem to be in a vacuum. The nose is reduced to a dot, and the mouth is a concave circle turned upward. The figure is wearing blue socks and green shoes. The arms are hanging down on either side of the body. The hands are poorly represented.

The Hand Drawing

There is a two minute latency. Danielle never looks at her own hands during this time or uses her hands as a model. She draws two average-sized hands (figure 3.46). They look like right hands. The nails are like portholes and the spaces between the fingers are all the same size. There are no wrinkles on the skin. The stroke is strikingly clean. The line is particularly interesting in that there are no corrections anywhere. The stroke "records" two lifeless hands.

Figure 3.45
Danielle's Childhood Drawing.

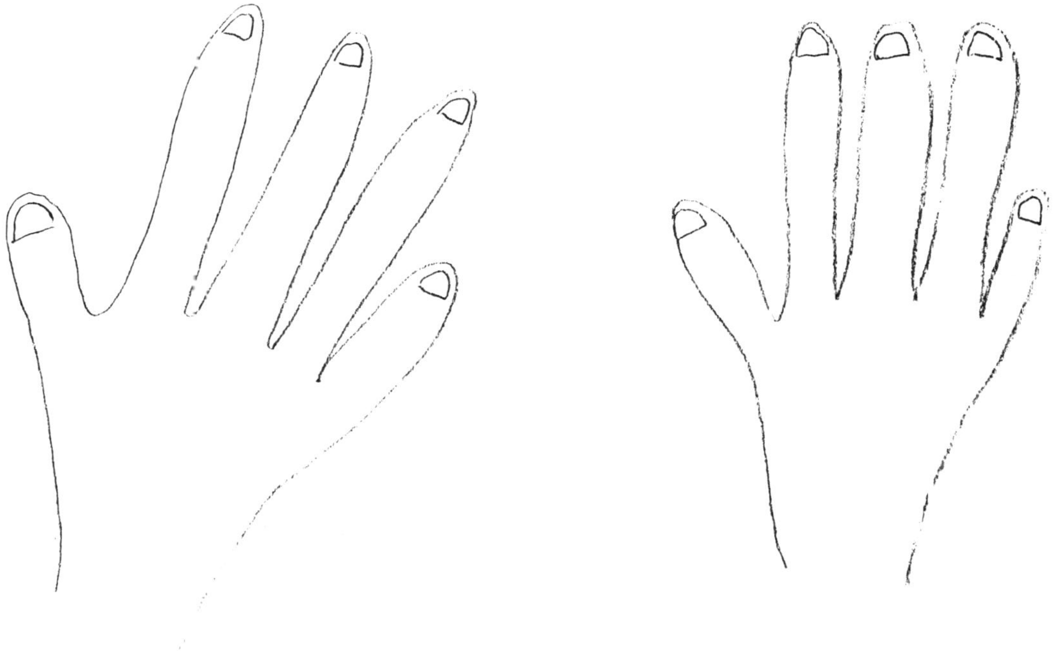

Figure 3.46
Danielle's Hand Drawing.

The hands appear impersonal and unrelated to the outside world.

The Hand That Disturbs

As soon as Danielle hears the instructions, she looks at her hands and starts drawing. The hand is reduced to a piece of a finger, a finger directed upward (figure 3.47). This single finger is "the hand that disturbs."

Inquiry

The Childhood Drawing: Danielle says she drew the house when she was eight. This house has *no limits*, as the sky and the roof blend into each other. This absence of limits, together with the confusion between outside and inside expresses confusion between the real body and the phantasmal body. Close examination of the first childhood drawing she made of a scarecrow figure shows that in fact the clothes are holding up the body. Color is applied like a mask over the figure. The figure is motionless, without a neck, and the shoulders start in the bottom of the face. Danielle claims she made this drawing when she was a child. If so, her lack of limits must date back to this period in time.

The Hand Drawing: Danielle makes no comments.

The Hand that Disturbs: Danielle says that it is her hand pointing at her and attacking her. The hand, reduced to one finger, reflects a fragmented body image, a self-aggressing one. Danielle was not interested in the hand drawing and

Figure 3.47
Danielle's Hand that Disturbs Drawing.

invested totally in the hand that disturbs. The latency and lack of comment on the hand drawing illustrate her lack of interest in body image. In contrast, Danielle looks at her own hands for the hand that disturbs. This hand is the active hand, attacking her. In her case, the hand is the bad object inside oneself, the bad instincts perceived as part of the self. There is no projection; rather there is a merging of persecution and persecutor.

Overall, the three drawings have psychotic features. Danielle's drawings may be emblematic of a schizophrenic CHaD. If Danielle actually produced drawings of this type at age eight, it might be particularly important to check for this type of drawing in children taking the CHaD.

COLOR BLIND

X is single, and about 60. He remembers making several childhood drawings, and offers to draw all of them.

The Childhood Drawing

X says he has trouble identifying colors because he is color blind. In fact, he names the whole row of colors he aligns on the top of the sheet correctly.

"When I was about 10, I had a boat that my mother and father bought in a hardware store (figure 3.48). *I dreamed about it. The sail was pieced together."* Then X. draws a bicycle. *"A bicycle with gears, the cyclist's leg is straight, and his foot is twice as big as the pedal. I put a helmet on him, he has red shorts, you can see a little red there, the helmet is red and yellow?"*

The third drawing is *"a house with an attic room, with green wooden shutters, a round window, a porch, the front door, let's say it's like that."*

"The smoke is grey?" (He checks.) *"I'm going to color that, the door is going to be black, the sides and the roof are going to be green."* X makes lengthy comments during the test. He apparently wants to disclose his anxiety when confronted with the test situation, or the feelings that apparently flood his defense system.

Figure 3.48
X's Childhood Drawing.

The Hand Drawing

X draws longitudinally from left to right, making fairly large hands (figure 3.49). The first hand has the palm concealed by fingers with nails. The wrist ends with a watchband. The palm of the second hand is also covered by fingers, but two fingers stuck together are pointing straight up. The palm ends in a curved line, without a wrist. The folds and knuckles stand out. In addition, this hand is completely colored green and purple. The third hand is shown in profile. The index finger is resting on the thumb and forms a hole. The stroke is hesitant, and the whole hand, with its unembellished wrist is shaded in grey.

The Hand That Disturbs

"You mean a hand and its function, since you want me to, I'll make a hand and its function. It's not easy to draw, a penis. Am I doing okay? It's a self-service hand." The hand, drawn in unsure strokes, is almost entirely covered by a penis with little bubbles coming out (figure 3.50).

Inquiry

The Childhood Drawing: X describes three fairly unrelated topics for his childhood drawing. There are a number of particularities in his choice of words: "my mother OR my father," the words "gear," "leg out straight," "red shorts," "you see a little red" (placed between the legs of the cyclist) "the door would be black." Thus, the colors that X claims he has trouble identifying in fact play a major role in his speech. The red and black that predominate are signs of anxiety and aggressivity.

The Hand Drawing: The most striking aspect of the hand drawing is its use of color. The second hand is green and purple. The third hand is almost black because of the skin lines that have been drawn. Color is rare in hand drawings and its usage is indicative of violence. As I have noted earlier, I have only observed color in pathological subjects, especially in individuals capable of killing or actual murderers. The strokes and lines used in the first hand are radically different

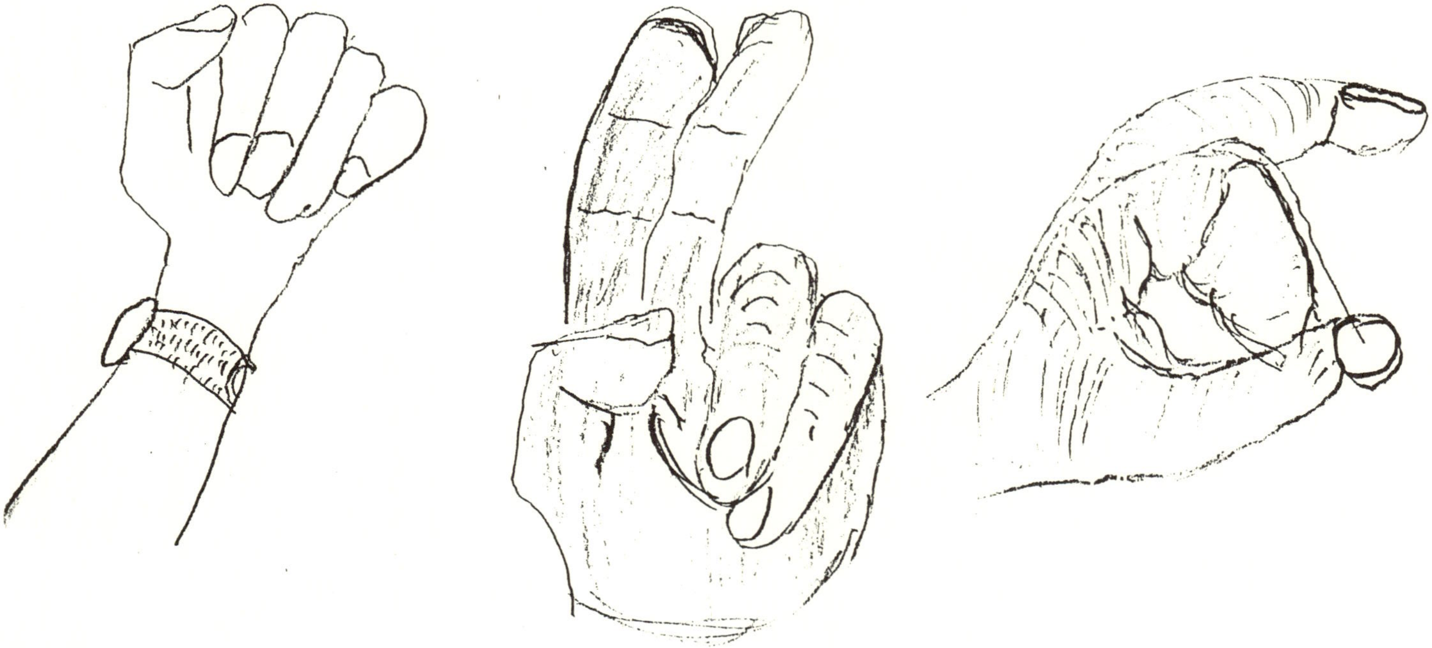

Figure 3.49
X's Hand Drawing.

Figure 3.50
X's Hand that Disturbs Drawing.

from the approach to the other two hands, as though the first hand was more "rational," more contained than the others. The broken lines in the second and third hands are indicative of anxiety. The stroke in the second hand is associated with their shape. The index and thumb form a hole and the hand with the two fingers raised looks like the obscene gesture children tend to make.

The Hand That Disturbs: The drawing simply confirms X's sexual problems. The instructions liberated X from his defenses. What was masked in the childhood and hand drawings (unrelated drawings, cut wrists, sexual form of the hands) is out in the open in the hand that disturbs. Why did this aggressivity emerge at the end of the test? One explanation is that it was not aimed at aggressing the examiner or amusing her, but rather was a request for violence itself to be interpreted. This hypothesis is confirmed by the use of color in the hands. Even though this person says he has trouble with color, nothing in his drawings or comments suggests that this is really the case. The violence in this man is obvious in all three drawings, and in fact all the hands folded over something were concealing his genitals. The brushy strokes used for the hand that disturbs are found primarily in impotent individuals. His explosion of violence takes the form of ejaculation. The case history of this patient reveals that he tried to strangle his mother on several occasions.

THE INTERLOCKING WEB

Y is a young Asian aged 21 who has been hospitalized because his family finds his behavior bizarre. He isolates himself, and the only time he talks is to insult his parents or spit in their faces. Y is a Vietnamese orphan adopted by a French couple who found him in the street when he was about ten.

The Childhood Drawing

Y plans to draw two army camps. He divides the sheet in two and starts to draw two tiny stick figures on either side and a tank. He then stops and says, "War is too sad, I'm going to do an abstract drawing." He turns the sheet over and starts by drawing a large figure on the left of the page with a round face. The black hair looks like a wig, parted in the middle. One hand is in a pocket, the left arm is hidden. He then draws a series of geometric interlocking shapes. Various unrelated objects are found in each shape: a night light, a ball (in fact a plane), a tree, a house, a person playing a violin (figure 3.51).

Then on a separate sheet of paper he draws a person, probably female, cross-legged like a Buddha with invisible hands (figure 3.52). The eyes are drawn in detail, with lashes; the hair is thick, embellished with a circle of tiny rectangles

Figure 3.51
Y's first Childhood Drawing; various unrelated objects and shapes.

Figure 3.52
Y's second Childhood Drawing; a (possibly female) Buddha image.

that look like a crown. The stroke is confident, there is no color.

The Hand Drawing

Y draws (from left to right) what is apparently a right hand and then the left (figure 3.53). He draws very slowly. The

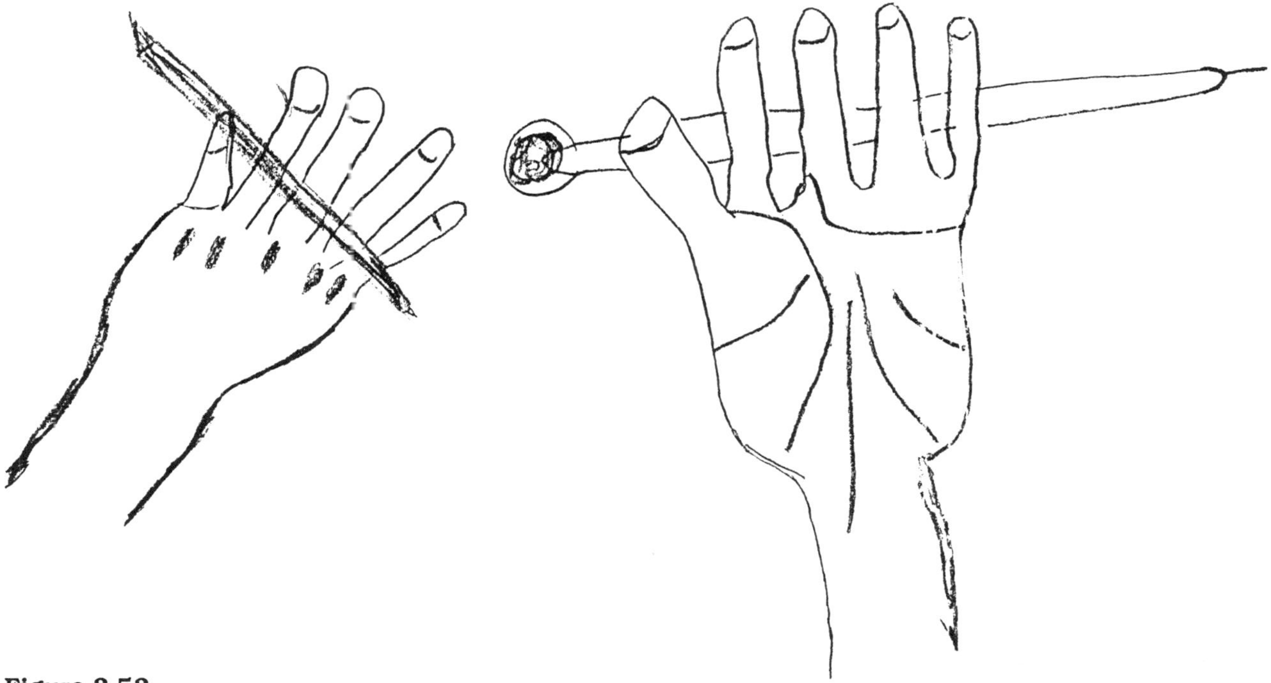

Figure 3.53
Y's Hand Drawing turned into his Hand that Disturbs Drawing. (He added the two "sticks" across the fingers of each hand.)

hands are average-sized. The hands are somewhat shapeless (small fingers, large knuckle bones). There are some palm lines. The left hand, although it is shown palm up, has nails.

The Hand That Disturbs

As soon as Y hears the instructions, he grabs his hand drawing and draws "sticks" across the fingers of each hand.

Inquiry and Comments

The Childhood Drawing: Y hardly speaks and does not date his childhood drawing. Initially he tries to draw a coherent scene, war, but he is soon overcome by the violence of his emotions. In the second drawing, he tries to control his libido by finding imaginary connections between unrelated objects (figure 3.51). The geometrical background, forming cells, resembles the drawings of children with severe anxiety.

When I ask him what he drew, he says, "It's a tree, a person, the owner's son plays the violin." I ask him what the plane is there for. He answers, "It's a picture, and the rest are roads." Everything seems as illogical and confused in Y's statements as the drawing. This lack of coherency is his parents' major concern. Y cannot or does not want to talk about himself.

The Hand Drawing and The Hand That Disturbs: The sticks for the hand that disturbs drawing were added to the hand drawing. One is inside the left hand, the other is outside the right hand. The hand drawing shows total confusion between inside and outside, container and content, since these hands cannot hold anything. The hand is represented by both the palm and the back of the hand. Y says the palm lines are veins. Careful examination of the hand with the palm down shows that the fingers are not connected to each other and that there is an open space between each finger. Y uses this same technique for the childhood drawing. He draws stick-fingers, which he does not connect to the hand on the right. The pinky on the left is cut off at the base of the finger.

This style of drawing where there are heteroclitic associations, a confusion between inside and outside, container and content, suggests psychosis. Did the war play a role in triggering this psychopathology? Or were there relational problems with strange people such as those in the two childhood drawings? The interlocking web doubtless conceals the secret of the intertwining of successive events experienced by this man.

Chapter 4

Clinical Interpretation of the CHaD

Two types of basic criteria may be used for clinical interpretation of the CHaD: general criteria concerning the examinee's behavior and comments, and specific criteria concerning the characteristics of each drawing.

Although each individual produces his or her own personal CHaD drawings, analysis across a large number of cases reveals certain regularities that can be used as guidelines for constructing a psychological profile. These regularities relate to latency, proportions, nature of stroke, type of hand and actions the hands perform, use of color, and recourse to writing. For a given individual, comparison and contrast of the general verbal and behavioral criteria with the specific graphic criteria provide a measure of internal coherency (see Tables 1 and 2).

INSTRUCTIONS AND ADMINISTRATION OF THE CHaD

The CHaD can be administered individually or in groups.

Materials

- Three sheets of white A4 paper (four sheets for children who will be asked to produce the free drawing), no tracing paper, no onion skin.

Table 1
Interpretation of the Normal Examinee

At all ages: Comparable latency for all instructions
Coherency between instructions, drawings and commentaries
Modulation of proportions and stroke

	C	H	D
Child	Ability to regress	Self-Concept	Self-Image (hand that is not drawing or picture of someone else)
Adolescent	Ability to regress Within boundaries	Self-Concept or Idol	No identification (someone else)
	Geometric figures or symbols		Often caracicatural (cartoons) Can distance self
Elderly	Ability to regress	Self-Concept	Identification or no identification
	Within boundaries Wobbly stroke, Small drawings		

- A black 2B pencil (medium), well sharpened. It is important to use this type of pencil for stroke analysis.
- A box of 12 crayons (or markers for children).
- A pencil sharpener.
- No eraser.

Testing and Examiner-Examinee Relationships

The psychologist should be in an office where he or she will not be disturbed during administration of the test. The examiner should sit next to (rather than facing) the examinee. No comments should be made on use of color. When examinees hesitate, they should be reminded that artistic abilities are not being measured. Individuals may use both

Table 2
Interpretation of the Pathological Examinee

At all ages: Significant increase in administration time
Differences in latencies across drawings
Lack of coherency between instructions, drawings and commentaries
Use of writing, numbers or esoteric symbols

	C	H	D
Child	C more advanced than FD	Active hands that touch or hit	Active hands depicting verbalization of violence
Adolescent and Adult	Confusion between inside/outside Loss of boundaries Very small or very large drawings	Long latency Very large or very small drawings Color	Rush to draw own hands Lack of distancing Fragmentation
Elderly	Accumulation of unrelated details	Fragmented or injured hands Calligraphy Loss of intent Illegible	Allegorical hands

sides of the sheet. Erasers and rulers are not allowed. If, however, the examinee uses the crayon as a ruler, the psychologist should not intervene. As soon as the drawing is finished, the examiner should remove it and write C for the Childhood Drawing, H for the Hand Drawing, D for the Hand that Disturbs, and FD for the Free Drawing. The placement and order of the hand drawings should also be noted.

Administration always adheres to the following order: the Childhood Drawing (C), the Hand Drawing (H), the Hand that Disturbs (D), and the Free Drawing (FD) exclusively for children.

The Childhood Drawing

The examinee is given a sheet of blank white paper, a black pencil, and a box of crayons (or markers for children). The instructions are as follows:

Adults: "Draw the drawing you made the most when you were a child." If the adult hesitates, add: "You can also draw a drawing from when you were a teenager." If the subject still hesitates, reassure him or her with generalities.

Children: "Draw the drawing you made the most when you were little." If the child hesitates, add, "when you were little in nursery school (primary school), you must have had a drawing you made often."

The Hand Drawing

The examinee is given a second sheet of blank white paper and a black pencil and is asked to draw hands, as many as he or she likes, in any position. Subjects are asked not to trace around their hands. The crayons remain on the table, but no mention is made of them.

The Hand That Disturbs

The examinee keeps the pencil. The box of crayons remains on the table. The subject is asked to draw the hand that disturbs, a hand that bothers him or her. If the examinee doesn't understand the instructions, they can be repeated, adding "draw the hand that disturbs *you*, the hand that bothers you." Above all, do not induce the response by mentioning a threatening hand or a hand that is frightening. If the subject traces around his or her hand, do not intervene.

The Free Drawing

After children have completed the first three CHaD drawings, they are asked to produce the drawing they make the most at the current time.

Coding During Administration

The psychologist takes notes during administration, which are used later for clinical interpretation. These notes include information on:

> Latency for each drawing (i.e., the time elapsed between the start of the instructions and the start of the drawing), and drawing time.

Spontaneous comments during each task.

Order of appearance of elements in the drawing. This order is highly informative as to:

- the examinee's way of working (orderly, disorderly, systematic, etc.).
- difficulties in producing the drawing (corrections, emphasis, trial and errors, etc.).
- hesitations (pauses) before going on with the drawing.

Inquiry

The inquiry is based on responses to a certain number of questions and on spontaneous comments during the drawings. Once the three or four drawings have been completed, the psychologist gives them back to the examinee in the following order: C, H, D, FD and records the subject's responses.

The Childhood Drawing: The examinees are asked 1) how old they were when they made this type of drawing and 2) whether the drawing corresponds to something particular in their childhood. (An associative context can be associated to the age at which they made their drawing. This may include moving, birth or death of a family member, etc.)

The Hand Drawing: The examinees are asked what the hands are doing.

The Hand That Disturbs: Examinees are asked 1) who the hand belongs to; 2) what the hand is doing; and 3) why it disturbs them.

Free Drawing: The children are asked to comment on the drawing if they want to.

After the specific inquiry, all subjects are asked to state which hand drawing they prefer. This is done in a specific way. The psychologist takes drawings 2 and 3 (H and D) and shows both of them to the subject. The subject is asked to state which she or he prefers and why.

GRAPHIC SPECIFICITIES

Latency

There is no reason to clock latency because the difference between normal and pathological subjects is obvious. The CHaD normally takes about ten minutes to complete. However, it can take twice or sometimes three times as long. Subjects tend either to rush into drawing or to exhibit long periods of latency (excluding individuals whose medication slows them down considerably). Once the instructions have been given, latency can be related to comprehension of the instructions or a hesitation regarding execution of the drawings (or both).

This comprehension and execution time may differ considerably for a given individual across drawings. A person may draw the childhood drawing rapidly and be extremely slow in drawing the hand drawings or vice versa. However, at all ages, an individual who has a great deal of trouble with strokes and lines, who presses down hard on the pencil, or who rectifies continually in such a meticulous way that the test takes an hour to complete is clearly pathological and obsessional.

Beyond the individual latencies for each drawing, the key to interpretating this factor is the comparison across drawings. Clearly, times vary across subjects, but three regularities stand out.

Regularities in Children

The maltreated child has longer latencies. The case histories show that in abused children latencies are long for the hand and the hand that disturbs drawings. Some children may be unable to execute these drawings because the sexual or violent connotations are so strong.

Nancy, for example, a 10 year old who drew her childhood drawing within the normal range of time, hesitated and finally refused to draw the hand drawing. After one minute of latency (which is long) and encouragement, she drew the hand that disturbs, saying it was hers. Children normally state that the hand that disturbs belongs to them, but in this case the attribution was strange because it came after a long latency and a refusal to draw the hand drawing. Analysis of the entire case shows that Nancy had been sexually abused by her father since the age of 5: the hands show sexual connotations which this little girl cannot overcome.

Regularities in Adults

Psychotics tend to present heterogeneous latencies. Schizophrenics tend not to understand the instructions for the hand drawing, in particular what "hands" mean. "Hand" is apparently too abstract for them and does not convey meaning. In contrast, as soon as these subjects hear the instructions for the hand that disturbs they rush to draw and generally trace around their own hands (fully or partially). Latency is very short for the hand that disturbs as compared to the hand or childhood drawings.

In other forms of psychosis, increased latency appears to be due to execution rather than to comprehension of the instructions. Psychotic subjects take an extremely long time representing minute (and often unrelated) details, or may focus on one single detail. Both execution time and patient comments are extremely long.

Regularities in the Elderly

Latency tends to be the longest for the childhood drawing. The elderly take enormous precautions before launching into drawing. As seen previously, the elderly do not tend to be confident and they complain that their childhoods are much too far away. Once initial reticence is overcome and the elderly person has been encouraged, however, there is no latency.

Proportions

The drawings "speak" through nervous or broken strokes or harmonious or clashing color (exclusively in the childhood and free drawings). This is why the same theme can take on a totally personal meaning in different individuals. Drawings are individualized by their proportions, the type and quality of the stroke, the choice of colors, and the use of writing.

At all ages, drawings can be large, average, or small. Large drawings are defined as occupying more than two-thirds of the total surface of the sheet; average drawings cover one-third to two-thirds of the sheet, and small drawings are entirely within a 9th to a 16th of the sheet.

Proportions in the Childhood Drawing

In children, most of the childhood drawings made by 3, 4, and 5-year-olds are large. In contrast, in the elderly, drawings tend to be small. In normal adults, the childhood drawing is average or large. Patients in psychiatric wards tend to produce extreme drawings that are either tiny or enormous. One case in point is a young woman who walks around naked, regardless of season. Her childhood drawing is a face, which she can hardly fit into the sheet. She uses the sheet vertically, and the long hair starts at the top and goes down to the bottom. In contrast, an anorexic, mute 32-year-old who thinks she is the devil (see case history of Z in Chapter 3) makes a tiny childhood drawing at the top left-hand corner of the sheet. It depicts a house and a vegetable garden with leeks and carrots. The garden is black and white and has a somber look, and the plants are in a row like tombs.

The size of the drawings may be the mirror image of the place people self-attribute in their relationships with others.

Proportions in the Hand Drawing

Normal subjects generally reveal several facets of their personalities and draw between one to four average-sized hands that are comparable or slightly disproportionate to each other, an indication of adaptation. The psychotic individual uses extremes, either very large or very small hands.

Proportions in the Hand That Disturbs

The normal subject tends to reproduce the proportions used in the Hand drawing. The psychotic subject tends to draw a very small hand that disturbs and reduces it even more by fragmentation (e.g. reducing the hand to one finger).

Stroke

In the Childhood Drawing

One particular type of stroke stands out in the Childhood drawings: "wire" stick people. This use of strokes to draw a person is rare and merits attention. The figure is totally stylized with two strokes for the arms, two strokes for the legs and a circle for an empty face (no facial characteristics). There is no hint of volume. This wire-figure person can be found at all ages and is often associated with death, the recent death of a relative or friend, or suicidal tendencies in the subject.

In the Hand Drawing

The CHaD interpretation is similar to descriptions and interpretations found in writers such as Kris (1952) or Hammer (1958). The stroke governs proportions, and the size of the drawing. It thus provides indications as to the individual's adaptation to reality. When the hand is too big, size may be an indication of immaturity, or lack of limits. When the hand is too small, the size may indicate inhibition.

Type of stroke may also reveal dominant psychological traits.

Wavering, spindly strokes provide cues to anxiety in the adult but are typical in the child and in the elderly. Differences in pressure are present in people who are well balanced. Thick, heavy, reinforced strokes are found in either fairly primary individuals or violent people. It tends to be found in psychiatric patients where it is sometimes associated with writing (calligraphy).

Repeated strokes over the same area occur when an individual overlays a line heavily. This is a pathological trait, which often has a functional origin.

Two kinds of strokes have major significance:

1. *A clean, uniform stroke with little pressure and no rectifications* where the result is obtained without lifting the pencil from the paper. This type of stroke emerges mainly in schizophrenics. These individuals may not be able to deviate from their lines or are locked into them. The lines are light, and the absence

of pressure creates a monotonous tone. Pfiester (1940) reported that in certain disorders including schizophrenia, there is low pressure and the stroke is faint, whereas individuals with functional disorders and epileptics use heavier pressure. Pfiester also reported a high degree of uniformity in pressure among catatonics and the mentally retarded.

2. *Dotted lines* have only been found in the CHaD in psychotic (and not schizophrenic) adults, and often correspond to a change in the patient's remarks, in particular more unrealistic statements.

Use of Color

Color in the Childhood Drawing

As in children's drawings, the colors used in the childhood drawing have major significance. Color tends to be used more in the childhood drawing than in the other CHaD drawings, regardless of age of examinee. In the very old, there is less use of color in the childhood drawing. This may be due to a decline in visual acuity, but also to the fact that crayons were a luxury in these people's childhoods. A childhood drawing in pencil has a sense of sadness to it, which can be related to pathologies in children, adolescents, and adults.

Color in the Hand Drawing

Color in the hand drawing is of extreme importance. It only emerges in examinees who have killed or are violent. Caution is required in interpretation, since it can reflect intent as well as acting out.

Use of Writing

One major feature of patients in psychiatric wards is the combined use of writing and drawing. Some of these patients state they do not remember their childhood drawings, and they draw faces composed of numbers. Others assign meaning to letters of the alphabet, which enable them to decipher the universe. (Some were even willing to share this knowledge with me, a gift of God according to them; see figure 4.1).

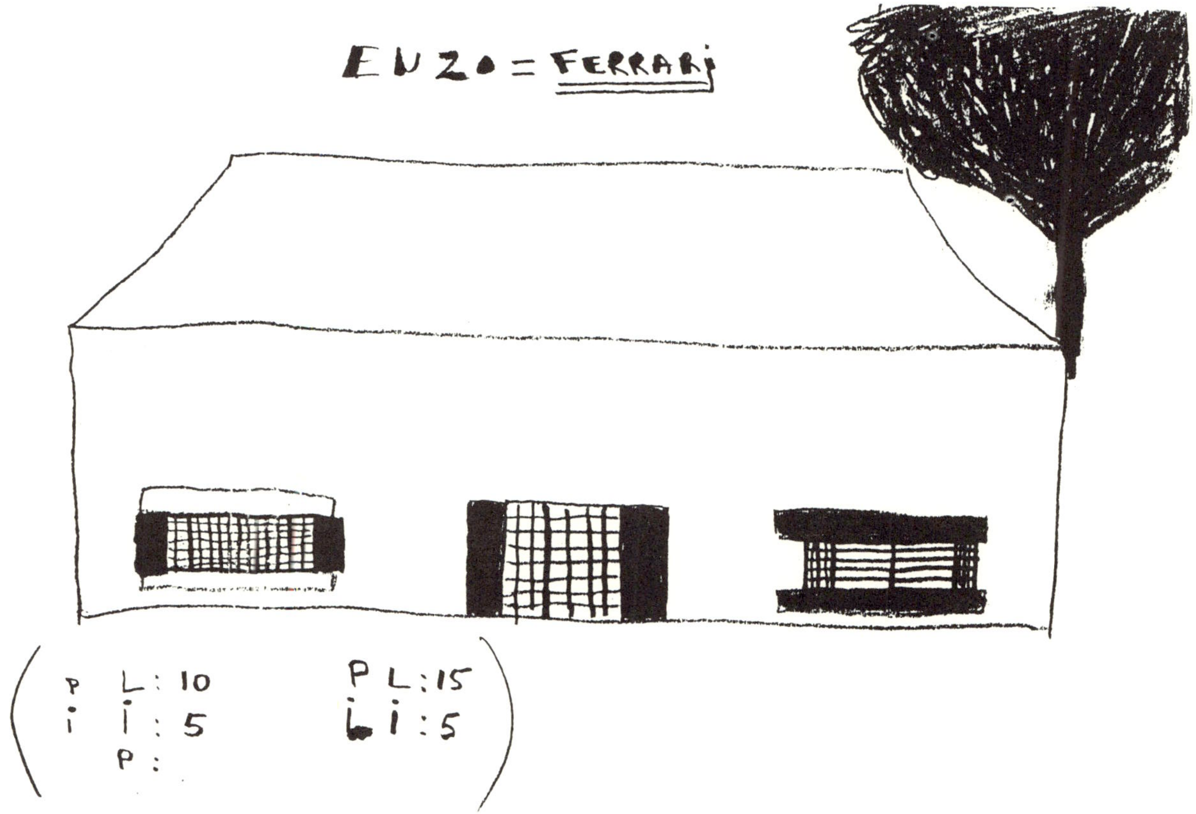

Figure 4.1
An example of the use of writing in the drawings of patients in psychiatric wards.

In this group of patients, the childhood and hand drawings are accompanied by unconventional signs, letters, numbers that have a meaning only to their authors. Letters and insignias are only rarely found in children's hand or hand that disturb drawings. One exception is the popular symbol of a hand in the handshake position for an antiracism campaign (in France) with the slogan inside, "don't touch my pal." When writing is present in children's drawings, there are often concomitant school adjustment and behavioral problems.

A distinction should be made between writing and signatures. Signing is frequent in children and adolescents, and is a very ordinary form of self-affirmation at these ages.

In senile adults, writing is extremely common. In this case, the writing is legible and comprehensible and it substitutes for the act of drawing itself. These subjects understand the instructions but apparently have a processing problem. This form of writing differs considerably from the esoteric output of psychiatric patients, yet it is striking that the ties between writing and drawing are present in both populations.

Coherency

Coherency is a prime determinant in interpreting the childhood drawing. Coherency in the hand and the hand that disturbs is connected to latency, that is, to the time the examinee takes to follow instructions and to recognize that the hands are an integral part of him- or herself or that they belong to others.

Coherency at All Ages

The first aspect of coherency is whether the topic the examinee states or wants to draw is recognizable in the finished product. Lack of coherency between drawing and commentary is a sign of pathology. In the "Interlocking Web" case history, for example (see Chapter 3), the story is so strange that the juxtaposition of unrelated details is arresting. This strange form can be found in the childhood drawing as well.

Take the case of Eugenia, aged 9 and a half, who is referred by her teacher to the psychologist for her poor grades and a "worrying attitude." In her childhood drawing, Eugenia combines a series of incoherent features that are unrelated to her commentary on the drawing. Eugenia draws a line of varied objects on a pedestal that could be a table. On either side are things that could be apples, a kind of large bowl with pebbles in it, and on the other side a plate with a knife and fork. Under the "table" are three trees in a row and to their left is a scribble that looks like a completed puzzle of a hand. In addition there are incongruities. Part of a face is sketched in one corner of the sheet. The hand drawings are unfinished. The only drawing that shows a form of coherency is in the hand that disturbs. Eugenia traces around her own hand, but she draws a horizontal line for the bottom of the nails, a nonanatomical feature. This child is highly disturbed, very fragile, or extremely sensitive.

Adult childhood drawings in pathological individuals may depict a series of superimposed drawings, like "short stories" arranged horizontally or vertically on the sheet. The themes are unrelated, except that the examinee states having made them at the same point in time in childhood. This type of drawing is commonly found in manic-depressives.

A 40-year-old doctor, for example, first draws the sea, then adds a boat, octopuses, and then suddenly draws a whole series of elements in the water that have nothing to do with the sea. He claims that he also drew this type of drawing at the same time and does not seem aware of the confusion on the paper. In the elderly, there are certain cases of disorientation and a juxtaposition of elements.

In normal subjects, people ask for several sheets of paper or use both sides of the paper to represent different drawings. Thus, the coherency of the drawing, reinforced by the coherency of the examinee's comments, provide cues to pathology.

The issue of the age at which a pathology first appeared can be assumed to be linked to the age at which the examinee states having drawn the childhood drawing. In the case of Eugenia for example, both the childhood drawing and the free drawing contained a mixture of themes. The fact of hearing that she was both normal and intelligent apparently had an impact because there were no more problems after she took the CHaD. Clearly, being "normal" requires skillful balance on the tightrope over any number of pathologies.

Today, Eugenia is able to produce a structured childhood drawing, although the stroke is unrectified and continuous. In contrast, her hand drawings are complete and harmonious, showing healthy integration of self concept.

Paradoxically enough, coherency in the childhood drawing should include defects. The overly perfect drawing, one made as if by a professional artist, is not always indicative of normalcy.

Chapter 5

Issues and Perspectives

The CHaD can be seen as a telescoped *curriculum vitae*, retracing the childhood of the examinee, revealing what he or she has become, and helping shed light on his or her future.

The real issue, of course, is the validity of the CHaD. Its simple and unspectacular instructions, its short administration time, and its age range (from 4 to 100+) may leave Cartesian spirits somewhat skeptical. The CHaD is not a novel laced with psychology. Rather, the literary dimension of storytelling forms the framework for interpretation and helps avoid oversimplified schemas and generalities.

The CHaD helps penetrate the personality of each examinee. Because the CHaD is individualized, it should not be viewed as a source of multiple histories, as numerous as there are cases. On the contrary, the CHaD situates each "case" on the human level, a level where there can be help and assistance.

The aim of any evaluation is to obtain an overall picture of the problems the individual is facing and to attempt to provide a solution to these problems. In this sense, the CHaD is like a physical examination since it furnishes indications on the symptom, the past history, and the meaning of the disorder.

It is always surprising to see to what extent people invest in the CHaD drawings. One key sign is examinees' steady gaze towards the psychologist: this is the point in time when precisely those questions the examinee wishes us to ask can at last be raised. The CHaD proves to the examinee that the psychologist is focused on the root of his or her personal issues and that the psychological examination he or she is undergoing can help. Examinees become cooperative at this juncture and ask for assistance in overcoming their suffering.

The CHaD diagnosis (or diagnoses) emerges from the intersection of the examinee's artwork and comments about them. The CHaD is not an intelligence test. It can serve to:

Obtain a quick case history.

Understand the issues the person is coping with as regards identity, whether this identity is fragmented.

Determine the degree of the examinee's autonomy as regards emotionality.

By responding or refusing to respond to the instructions, and being able or unable to project into the past (childhood drawing), the present (hand drawing), and the future (hand that disturbs), the examinee reveals his or her potential for adaptation and his or her personality profile. The CHaD elicits intention, motivation, and libidinal dynamics from the individual when confronted with his or her body image, self, and others. He or she provides a demonstration of ability to handle emotions.

The childhood drawing provides the frame for the case history, or rather the personalized history of each examinee. Who was he? When did he make the drawing? How did he relate to his family circle? How did he relate to others? Which other people?

When an individual assigns a date to a drawing, he reveals the age and the conflict that was the turning point of his life.

The hand drawing and the hand that disturbs, which are direct projections of body image, shed more light on individual identity. How is the body experienced? Is it fragmented or whole?

Other tests can respond to these inquiries, in particular the Rorschach. An ongoing correlational study suggests that there are high positive relationships between the CHaD and the Rorschach for the identification of disorders and potential violence. The CHaD, unlike the Rorschach, can be used early on in treatment, even during severe crises.

The CHaD provides current data as a supplement to the patient's past history. It can rapidly identify whether the examinee has a psychotic or a neurotic profile, and in the latter case it can give some indications as to cause.

The CHaD is particularly suited to two groups of individuals: children and the elderly. The CHaD is helpful in the case of maltreated or sexually abused children in that these children tend to be mute and this creates a real obstacle in other tests. Phallic drawings in the CHaD are not exclusively interpreted in terms of abuse. Furthermore, children often exhibit destructuration, yet it is difficult to know why. The CHaD, by creating a nonthreatening environment, enables the child to better express the origins of a problem.

In the elderly, the CHaD helps overcome communication problems and clichés such as "the final shot." The CHaD can:

> Reveal incipient intellectual deterioration, even before there are other clinical signs of disease such as Alzheimer's. This may be of great interest when a treatment has been found.
>
> Help determine whether apparent senility is masking severe depressive tendencies.

METAMORPHOSIS

We enjoy stories as adults because our search for the marvelous, instilled in childhood, is still part of us. We still wait for that wonderful moment when the beast turns into a handsome prince. The themes observed in CHaD protocols draw on this notion of metamorphosis. In the Childhood drawing, adult examinees become "little" again, although they know that they are "big." Even a 4-year-old can understand that, "Now I am big but when I was little. . . ." As though touched by a magic wand, the examinee can return once again to a vanished world.

In the childhood drawing, there is a regression to the extent that the individual returns to early automatic responses, primary processes, a narcissistic refuge for the ego when the first wound was inflicted. The time of the childhood drawing is an Eden preceding all elaboration or restructuration of the ego. It is the time before frustrations, the last known paradise. The childhood drawing represents Adam and Eve before the Fall. Most childhood drawings represent bucolic scenes, landscapes, flowers, and shiny clean houses with no human figures.

The magic operates at its best in the hand that disturbs, where examinees are granted their wish to see their worst nightmares take shape in the form of a hand that metamorphosizes into a monstrous creation, amputated of its fingers, twisted, gnarled, with pointed witch's nails or Dracula's grasp. Just as in fairy tales, the hand that disturbs is a frightening hand, one that rekindles what were thought to be the extinct fears of childhood.

The strength of fairy tales lies in their appeal to our primitive fears, our fear of encountering the wicked witch who will cast a spell and transform us into a toad or some other horrifying creature. This fear is so deeply rooted that normal subjects always interpret the instructions to draw the hand that disturbs as a threatening hand, belonging to someone other than themselves. We know that the distance between the hand that disturbs and the examinee's own life is indicative of the ability to distance oneself from suffering. A witch's hand with long nails can be a witch for one examinee or the unspeakable to another person, that is, the person him- or herself. The psychotic realizes that the hand that disturbs is his or her own hand, as though no transformation, no metamorphosis were possible any longer. The wicked witch casts her spell, and the examinee has been metamorphosized into the "bad object." In short, the pathological individual is one who has not been able to escape the witches of collective memories that stem from our childhoods.

References

Anzieu, D. *Le Moi-Peau*, Paris: Dunod, 1985.

Chauchard, P. *Le Cerveau et la Main Créatrice*, Neuchâtel, Switzerland: Delachaux et Niestlé, 1970.

Davido, R. *La Découverte de Votre Enfant par le Dessin*, Paris: Nouvel Office d'Edition, 1971.

Davido, R. *Le Langage du Dessin d'Enfant*, Paris: Presses de la Renaissance, 1976.

Davido, R. "Le Dessin de la Main: Propositions pour une Reflexion projective." Ph.D. diss. University of Paris VII, 1985.

Davido, R., C. Moreaux, and D. Krukoff. "Le Childhood Hand that Disturbs et son utilisation chez les sujets atteints de maladie d'Alzheimer ou de type Alzheimer." In *Alzheimer Actualities*, Paris: IPSEN, 40 (1990).

Davido, R., C. Moreaux, and A. Baulon. "Le CHaD Test, Animation dans un service de long séjour," in *Gérontologie et Société*, 66 (1993): 83-89.

Freud, S. *Psychopathology of Daily Life*, Standard Edition XIV 310, 1901.

Freud, S. *Mourning and Melancholia*, In *Metapsychology*, 1917. New York: Penguin, 1973.

Hammer, E.F. *The Clinical Application of Projective Drawings*, Springfield, Ill.: Charles C. Thomas, 1958.

Kris, E. *Psychoanalytic Explorations in Art*, New York: International Univiversity Press, 1952.

Palau i Fabre, J. *Picasso, Dessins pour ses Enfants*, Barcelona: Poligrafa, 1966.

Parmelin, H. *Picasso Dit*, Paris: Gonthier, 1966.

Pfiester, H. In Anastasi A. and J. Foley, "A Survey of the Literature on Artistic Behavior in the Abnormal," *Psychological Monographs* 52, no. 71 (1940).

Powell, K. "Characteristic Features of Two Diagnosis Groups of the Hand That Disturbs You, The Third Part of the CHaD Projective Test." Ph.D. diss., Rosebridge Graduate School of Integrative Psychology, Walnut Creek, California, 1988.

Prévost, C. M., and R. Davido. "Le CHaD Projective Drawing Test," *Bulletin de Psychologie*, 44 (1991): 402.

Rank, O. "Don Juan and His Double" (1914–22), In Harry Tucker, *The Double*, Chapel Hill: University of North Carolina Press, 1971.

Index

About the Author

ROSELINE D. DAVIDO received her doctorate in Clinical Psychopathology and Psychoanalysis from the University of Paris. Her earlier books are *La Découverte De Votre Enfant Par Le Dessin* (1971) and *Le Langage Du Dessin D'Enfant* (1976).

ISBN 0-275-94417-4
90000>
EAN
9 780275 944179
HARDCOVER BAR CODE